Business Intelligence Competency Centers

Business Intelligence Competency Centers

A Team Approach to Maximizing Competitive Advantage

GLORIA J. MILLER

DAGMAR BRÄUTIGAM

STEFANIE V. GERLACH

WILEY

John Wiley & Sons, Inc.

Published by John Wiley & Sons, Inc. Hoboken, New Jersey.

Published simultaneously in Canada

For general information on our other products and services, or technical support, please contact our Customer Care Department within the United States at 800-762-2974, outside the United States at 317-572-3993 or fax 317-572-4002.

Wiley also publishes its books in a variety of electronic formats. Some content that appears in print may not be available in electronic books.

For more information about Wiley products, visit our Web site at *http://www.wiley.com.*

Library of Congress Cataloging-in-Publication Data

Miller, Gloria J.
    Business intelligence competency center : a team approach to maximizing competitive
        advantage / Gloria J. Miller, Dagmar Brautigam, Stefanie V. Gerlach.
            p. cm.
    Includes index.
    ISBN-13: 978-0-470-04447-6 (cloth)
    ISBN-10: 0-470-04447-0 (cloth)
    1. Business intelligence—Management.   2. Knowledge management.   3. Strategic
planning.   I. Brautigam, Dagmar.   II. Gerlach, Stefanie Virginia, 1969–.   III. Title.
    HD38.7.M547 2006
    658.4′72—dc22

                                                                        2006003355

Printed in the United States of America

10 9 8 7 6 5 4 3

About the Authors

Gloria J. Miller, Vice President, Professional Services Division, SAS International, heads the international Professional Services Division at SAS, is the executive manager for the development of SAS Industry Intelligence Solutions, and is on the board of directors of SAS Global Services. Throughout her career of more than 18 years in the information technology industry, Miller has received accolades for her skills in the management and delivery of IT systems and programs and in software development and support.

She holds a master's degree in Business Administration from Bowie State University in Bowie, Maryland, and a Bachelor of Science degree from Augusta State University in Augusta, Georgia.

Dagmar Bräutigam, Professional Services Program Manager, SAS International, has led the development of the Business Intelligence Competency Center Program and the Information Evolution Assessment Service. Based in Heidelberg, Germany, she is responsible for creating, developing, and rolling out SAS' education and consulting programs and services for the SAS Europe, Middle East, and Africa and the Asia/Pacific regions. Bräutigam studied translation sciences in Heidelberg, London, and Geneva, and holds a degree from Ruprecht-Karls-University of Heidelberg.

Dr. Stefanie V. Gerlach, Senior Program Consultant, SAS International, has extensive experience in developing training programs for project teams and end users. She is responsible for developing the Business Intelligence Competency Center initiative for SAS. She is responsible for creating, developing, and rolling out the Business Intelligence Competency Center Services for the SAS Europe, Middle East, and Africa and the Asia/Pacific regions. Gerlach has studied political science, history, and Protestant theology in Heidelberg and Paris, and holds a Ph.D. in Political Science from Ruprecht-Karls-University of Heidelberg. Gerlach also codeveloped a manual that describes training methods and how to implement and manage computer training.

About the Contributors

The main authors would like to thank the following individuals for their invaluable contributions. Without them, this book would not have been possible.

The table below details the chapters they contributed to.

Chapter 1	Chapter 7
Eleanor Taylor	*John Davies*
	Frank Leistner
	Britta Lerch
Chapter 2	**Chapter 8**
Pamela Prentice	*Achim Granzen*
Chapter 3	**Chapter 9**
Hannu Ritvanen	*Hannu Ritvanen*
Chapter 4	
Michael Nielsen	
Chapter 5	
Hannu Ritvanen	
Chapter 6	
Achim Granzen	

John Davies is a Senior Learning and Organizational Development Consultant for SAS International in Heidelberg, Germany. Davies directs Performance Management and Learning and Development initiatives for Professional Services in the SAS Europe, Middle East, and Africa region and consults on Change Management. He studied management and organizational development in the United Kingdom and Germany, and is a member of the Charted Institute of Personnel and Development.

Achim Granzen is a Senior Professional Services Specialist with SAS International Professional Services. In this role, Granzen ensures successful delivery and implementation of the SAS®9 architecture by providing training, conducting project planning and reviews, and creating methodologies and best practices for project estimation and implementation. Granzen holds a master's degree in Physics from Mercator University in Duisburg, Germany.

Frank Leistner is the Chief Knowledge Officer for SAS International. He leads worldwide SAS Knowledge Management initiatives, enabling SAS staff around the world to share knowledge and expertise about SAS products, methods, and processes for internal and external projects. With more than 12 years of experience in Knowledge Management, Leistner is a regularly invited speaker regarding Knowledge Management topics and is involved in a Harvard Round Table at the Harvard Learning Innovations Laboratory. Leistner holds a masters degree in Computer Science from Technical University Carolo-Wilhelmina at Brunswick, Germany, and an M.S. degree in Computer Science from the State University of New York (SUNY) at Albany.

Britta Lerch is a Team Leader, Knowledge Office Operations, with SAS International. Her key area of responsibility focuses on Knowledge Management, including planning and designing SAS knowledge systems, supporting the systems, managing content, and assessing and measuring implementation of Knowledge Management systems and processes worldwide. Lerch holds a Masters degree in Mathematics (German Diploma) from Technical University, Darmstadt in Darmstadt, Germany.

Michael Nielsen is a Senior Consultant for SAS International. Based in Copenhagen, Denmark, Nielsen has played a key role in the development of the Information Evolution Model and the Information Evolution Assessment Service, working closely with industry analyst groups as well as internal and external thought leaders. He is responsible for creating, developing, and rolling out the Information Evolution Assessment Service for the SAS Europe, Middle East, and Africa and the Asia/Pacific regions. Nielsen holds a degree in Economic and Information Science from the Aarhus School of Business, Aarhus, Denmark.

Pamela Prentice is a Senior Manager of Market Research for SAS. She directs efforts to gather and analyze information about software and technology markets to assist in the development of effective marketing strategies and sound business decisions. Prentice holds a degree in English from Jacksonville University, Jacksonville, Florida; an M.B.A in Marketing from the University of Mississippi; and is currently pursuing a Ph.D. in Marketing from the University of Mississippi, Oxford, Mississippi.

Hannu Ritvanen is a Business Consultant with SAS, based in Oy, Finland. With over 20 years experience in using SAS, Ritvanen helps SAS customers develop successful strategies for their Business Intelligence implementation, including process definition and management, systems architecture design, and organizational management. Ritvanen holds an M.Sc. (Ecom). degree in Economics from the Swedish School of Economics and Business Administration and is currently pursuing a Ph.D. in Stakeholder Dependency and Corporate Performance at the Swedish School of Economics and Business Administration in Helsinki, Finland.

Eleanor Taylor is a Senior Marketing Strategist with SAS. Taylor specializes in Business Intelligence, ensuring that SAS' Business Intelligence products and services meet the current and future needs for SAS customers. Taylor holds a degree in Sociology from Southern Illinois University in Carbondale, Illinois, and is currently pursuing a master's degree in Organizational Design from DePaul University in Chicago, Illinois.

Contents

Foreword

The world of Business Intelligence (BI) is changing, and the ideas in this book can help organizations address the transition. Business Intelligence has been with us (under several different names) for several decades, and one could argue that it has always been useful. However, in the past it has also been somewhat "marginal"—addressed to important but somewhat esoteric business problems, and rarely visible either to senior executives or to external customers or business partners. There clearly have been exceptions to this pattern, but for the most part BI and its practitioners have dwelled in the "back rooms" of organizations.

For an increasing number of organizations today, however, this is no longer the case. Based on research supported by SAS and Intel, I have concluded that the leading edge of BI involves companies in which analytics are central to their strategy and competitive advantage. These firms and organizations have employed sophisticated analytics and fact-based decision making to drive and support competition based on one of several possible strategic capabilities. The retailers Wal-Mart and Amazon, for example, have used analytics to optimize supply chain management. Travel and entertainment firms such as Harrah's and Marriott have used analytics to support customer loyalty and revenue management. In the financial services industry, Capital One and Progressive have focused on the analysis-based pricing and marketing of their products. In professional sports, the Oakland A's, Boston Red Sox, and New England Patriots have employed analytical approaches to selecting and compensating human resources—their very expensive players.

In these organizations, analytics and BI have escaped the back room for the boardroom. They are highly visible capabilities that get mentioned in annual reports and analyst briefings. Companies do not become analytical competitors without the urging and close attention from the senior executive suite. These firms have reached the ultimate stage in the SAS "information evolution model" described in this book: They are not only optimizing their business processes, but also creating innovation in products, services, and business models.

Of course, the emergence of analytical competition raises the question of how companies can build the necessary analytical capabilities. As this book suggests, based on survey results of how BI is managed now, most organizations today do not even handle the back-office BI role well. And even those analytical competitors I have found in my research typically took many years to build their analytical muscle; a faster route to success is needed. But the changes required to compete on numbers are both broad and deep. Serious analytical competition requires more than the traditional BI tools of hardware, software, and data. Substantial changes in organizational culture, employee behaviors and skills, and managerial decision styles will also be required. Some group within analytically focused organizations must take on the task of facilitating the development of the required BI capabilities.

That is where the primary subject of this book—the Business Intelligence Competency Center, or BICC—comes in. There is no better candidate organization to ensure that the requisite BI tools are available, to educate and train managers and users on analytical techniques and decision making, and to work with executives to ensure that BI supports the company's business strategy. Of course, BICCs can be useful even if BI plays only a support role in how a company competes. But creating such a center—whether it is called a BICC or something else—is absolutely critical when a company is attempting to make analytics a strategic weapon.

Here I won't go into the details on how to organize a BICC or the specific functions that should be included in one. The rest of this book has plenty of useful content of that sort. My point here is only to point out the essential role of the BICC in analytical competition and to alert readers to the highest and best use of this new organizational entity. Establishing a BICC is a good idea if you are doing any sort of Business Intelligence. However, if you use a BICC only to support a back-office BI approach, your organization is leaving a lot on the table, and it may be difficult to get the needed resources from senior management to embed BI into the organization's most strategic processes and capabilities. The most successful and strongly supported BICCs will be those that enable a new wave of analytical competition. In these environments, the return on investment in the BICC will be the growth and profitability of the entire enterprise. It would be competitively foolhardy not to endow such an important institution with all the support and resources it requires for a long and fruitful life span.

Tom Davenport

Preface

Purpose

This book advises organizations on how to set up and run Business Intelligence Competency Centers (BICCs). The book was developed to provide an overview of the BICC concept and its benefits and to give recommendations for BICC setup and maintenance.

Who Should Read This Book

This book has been written for anyone interested in the concept of BICCs and in how to plan, set up, and run them. The suggested audience includes the potential executive sponsor, information technology management, the business units that will be supported by the BICC, as well as the team of individuals tasked with the work of setting up the BICC and the individuals actually manning the BICC.

Depending on your role and interest, you might want to focus on specific sections in this book. The table below contains recommendations about which chapters will be of most interest to you.

The BICC Book Web Site

This book contains some checklists, job role descriptions, and other tools that you might find useful to have in electronic format. You can download these items from the SAS Web site. Note that the Web site is protected; you will need to use this login information:

URL: www.sas.com/bicc/book

User Name: bicc

Password: moreinfo

Note also that you must enter both user name and password in lowercase.

	Executive Sponsor	IT Management	Business Representative	BICC Setup Team and BICC Staff
Chapter 1 Introduction	X	X	X	X
Chapter 2 Business Intelligence in the Organization	X		X	X
Chapter 3 Primary Functions of the BICC	X	X		X
Chapter 4 Planning a BICC: Using the Information Evolution Model	X	X	X	X
Chapter 5 Human Capital				X
Chapter 6 Knowledge Processes				X
Chapter 7 Culture	X	X	X	X
Chapter 8 Infrastructure		X		X
Chapter 9 Setting Up and Ensuring Ongoing Support		X		X
Chapter 10 Cases from the Field	X		X	X
Chapter 11 Ten Recommendations for a Highly Effective BICC	X	X	X	X

Acknowledgments

The authors would like to thank the SAS customers who shared their BICC experiences: CSI-Piemonte, KBC, Mutual & Federal, and Nedbank.

A considerable number of people were involved in the creation of this book. In addition to acknowledging the contributions from SAS offices worldwide, the authors would like to extend special thanks to Peter Bennett (SAS International), Bruce Bond-Myatt (SAS South Africa), Werner Bundschuh (SAS International), Ana López Echevarria (SAS International), Paul Higgins (SAS International), Steven Ing (SAS Asia/Pacific), Norbert Seibel (SAS Germany), and Victoria Vaca Núñez (SAS International) for their invaluable comments and constructive input during the review process, as well as to David Lambert, Kerstin Lambert, and Nicole Trick (all of SAS International) for their research work.

Thanks also to Bettina Baumhauer and Stephanie Pauler (both of SAS International) for their assistance with the graphics, and to Alec Bews, Eric van Gendt, and Gracy Poelman (all of SAS Belgium), to Veronica Hodgson and Hanlie Myburg (both of SAS South Africa), and to Augusta Longhi (SAS Italy) for their help with the case studies.

This book would not have been possible without the continuous support and hard work from the production team, which included Caroline Brickley, Patrice Cherry, Monica McClain, and Julie Platt (all of SAS Americas) and Jeremy Collin (SAS International).

About SAS

SAS is the market leader in providing a new generation of business intelligence software and services that create true enterprise intelligence. SAS solutions are used at more than 40,000 sites, including 96 of the top 100 companies in the FORTUNE Global 500®, to develop more profitable relationships with customers and suppliers; to enable better, more accurate and informed decisions; and to drive organizations forward. SAS is the only vendor that completely integrates leading data warehousing, analytics and traditional BI applications to create intelligence from massive amounts of data. For nearly three decades, SAS has been giving customers around the world *The Power to Know*®.

Please contact your local SAS office for more information regarding Business Intelligence Competency Centers: http://www.sas.com/offices

Introduction

OVERVIEW

Business Intelligence is reaching more and more constituents inside and outside your organization. Information demands, data volumes, and audience populations are growing and will continue to grow exponentially. As the demand increases, so does the imperative for a sound strategy that meets your short-term needs and that provides the foundation to meet your long-term vision.

Current spending is changing focus from products that help control costs to those that can help grow the business.

Key Questions

Are you thinking about how to get the most out of BI? Are you wondering how to best sustain your investment in BI? Do you worry about how to ensure that every business decision made in your organization is backed up by the correct information? Are you asking yourself how to implement a comprehensive BI strategy that supports organizational goals and addresses the information requirements from the business? Do you wonder how to get information when you are sure the data must be there, but you do not know how to get a meaningful report?

BICC Concept

More and more organizations are forming a Business Intelligence Competency Center (BICC) as an answer to those questions. Gartner Research (www.Gartner.com) defines a BICC as a cross-functional team with specific tasks, roles, responsibilities, and processes for supporting and promoting the effective use of Business Intelligence across the organization. The hope is that a BICC can act as a center of expertise for Business Intelligence and drive and support its use throughout the organization. This more holistic approach to BI encompasses more than just the technology—it is part of an overall BI strategy that addresses these organizational dimensions:

- *Human capital:* The people tasked with delivering BI to the business and the business users consuming BI (see Chapter 5)
- *Knowledge processes:* The processes required for information to flow through the organization in the right way (see Chapter 6)

- *Culture:* How organizational culture affects the use of BI and how it is affected by the use of BI (see Chapter 7)
- *Infrastructure:* The technology used for BI (see Chapter 8)

While the concept of a BICC sounds very straightforward, the details might not be so easy to tackle. This book is designed to help you establish a BICC effectively. It describes the BICC concept, explores benefits and potential pitfalls, and looks at what you need to consider when setting up a BICC. In doing so, it examines the above-mentioned dimensions of human capital, knowledge processes, culture, and infrastructure. It provides you with a plan for the BICC setup and advice on the functions and roles required in a BICC. The book also details how a BICC can best work together with software vendors and contains some descriptions of BICC implementations.

Business Intelligence as a Competitive Differentiator

Like most organizations today, your organization measures success in many different ways, and those measures vary greatly from industry to industry. But for every business in every industry, revenue growth remains the most fundamental indicator—and by far the most critical.

Unfortunately, marketplace realities are making revenue targets harder and harder to reach. This tenuous environment is placing a huge premium on the ability to focus scarce resources in every corner of your organization on the strategies and tactics most likely to result in success. To gain this focus, your organization must infuse strategic and tactical decisions with the knowledge necessary to maximize revenue, reduce costs, minimize risk, and achieve competitive advantage.

What Is Business Intelligence?

Business Intelligence is defined as getting the right information to the right people at the right time. The term encompasses all the capabilities required to turn data into intelligence that everyone in your organization can trust and use for more effective decision making.

Business Intelligence is the one true source of sustainable competitive advantage. It allows your organization to drive revenues, manage costs, and realize consistent levels of profitability. An "intelligent enterprise"—one that uses BI to advance its business—is better able to predict how future economic and market changes will affect business, and such an organization is better poised to adapt and thrive under those new conditions to foster a culture of innovation and adaptation.

Business Intelligence Versus Gut Feel

The key to this vital knowledge lies in the mountains of raw data your organization already collects. Business Intelligence uncovers innumerable competitive advantages by transforming that raw data into actionable intelligence and by creating knowledge to implement winning strategies and deliver information that can be leveraged by your entire organization.

One of the greatest inhibitors to competitive advantage is acting solely on "gut feel" or "intuition." So many decisions have been made based on what someone feels versus what the data say. These decisions cannot be measured. They cannot be repeated. They cannot be easily understood or shared. Many domain experts have specialized knowledge and this knowledge and context needs to be joined with the data to improve future decision making and provide competitive advantage. Unstructured content needs to be considered as part of the overall information architecture.

Hindsight Versus Insight

Many organizations have adopted BI applications, in the hopes of extracting greater insights from all the data generated by their operational and transactional systems. Unfortunately, even after acquiring traditional BI, true competitive differentiation often remains elusive. One reason is that the competition is probably doing the same thing, with the same tools.

Furthermore, hindsight query and reporting—the typical offering that is labeled as "Business Intelligence"—cannot deliver the predictive insight and deep understanding that is required to outperform the pack. Past trends tend to be poor predictors of future possibilities. Organizations need a way to distill predictive insights from a multitude of interrelated factors, far beyond simple trend analysis. Otherwise, revenue opportunities might reveal themselves too late for positive action—or it might not be possible, given current processes, to mobilize resources quickly enough to take advantage.

If a BI solution cannot help you make sound decisions about your organization's future—easily, reliably, and at every level of the organization—it is neither good business nor intelligent. How can your organization leverage these advancements for competitive advantage? How can you best support your corporate strategy with a BI strategy that advances the business on a continuous basis? Who in your organization is going to be entrusted with that task? What opportunities will innovations like radio frequency identification (RFID) mean to your organization? And finally, how do you achieve more with less—more intelligence for the organization at less cost? The answer—at least in part—lies in establishing a Business Intelligence Competency Center.

Criteria for True Business Intelligence

According to SAS (www.sas.com), the leader in providing a new generation of business intelligence software and services, definition, a platform does not offer true Business Intelligence unless it satisfies all of these criteria:

- *Breadth. It integrates functions and technologies from across the organization.* Truly integrated BI integrates data from every corner of the organization—from operational/transactional systems, multiple databases in different formats, and all contact channels. The information flow can then transcend functional silos, organizational boundaries, computing platforms, and specialized tools.

- *Depth. It reaches all who need it, in a way that is relevant to them.* A true BI solution provides appropriate interfaces and tools for users at different levels of the organization, who have profoundly different needs. The results of analysis should be easily disseminated across all functional areas and organizational levels, so everyone can contribute to the organization's success.

- *Completeness. It is a comprehensive, end-to-end platform.* Business Intelligence success does not just happen at the application layer. And it is not just query and reporting. It depends on a chain of applications and technologies working together from a common data foundation to create a single, verifiable version of the truth.

- *Advanced analytics. It delivers predictive insights, not just hindsight.* Online Analytical Processing (OLAP) is a valuable part of the picture, but it is not your optimum source of competitive differentiation. Historical query and reporting—what many vendors call "BI"—merely tells you where the organization has been. Going beyond BI requires predictive analytics, such as forecasting, scenario planning, optimization, and risk analysis.

- *Data quality. It gives applications one validated, verified version of the facts.* Data are vital to the decision-making process, and ensuring that you have the *right* data is imperative. All major information technology (IT) analysts recognize the importance of data quality to the return on BI investment, yet many organizations are restricted by their choice of solution.

- *Intelligence storage. It meets the information needs of intelligence applications.* The data storage platform must be able to draw on information from many sources, prepare it for analysis, and deliver it quickly to the applications and platforms that need it.

However, BI is not just about software. Many BI projects fail because no provisions are made for a sustainable environment for BI, which includes the appropriate processes, the people with in-depth BI skills, and an organizational culture that fosters fact-based decision making.

BUSINESS INTELLIGENCE COMPETENCY CENTER

Six Challenges in Exploiting Business Intelligence

Increasingly, organizations are realizing that there is more to BI than simply employing technology. There is a need for a comprehensive, strategic approach to BI that addresses technology as well as human capital, knowledge processes, and culture. Without strategy, the results are inconsistent BI deployments; difficulties in managing, implementing, and supporting BI initiatives that span multiple departments; and a lack of standardization of methodologies, definitions, processes, tools, and technologies as well as insufficient BI skills. These challenges can be defined in six categories:

Data challenges

Technology challenges

Process challenges

Strategy challenges

Users challenges

Cultural challenges

Data Challenges. Data are at the heart of all BI initiatives. The data required and the time and effort necessary to collect the necessary data and to ensure their accuracy are often underestimated. Data issues typically are the leading cause of failure and the most costly element of BI implementations. It takes a lot of time, resources, and effort to identify, map, and create the necessary rules and processes to ensure that the data are being used consistently and accurately across the organization, promoting a single version of the truth.

The many disparate data sources usually do not "speak" to each other, and each might be owned and managed by different groups that report to different organizational entities. In many cases, just getting to the data is extremely labor intensive, and there is no assurance that the data will be accurate or timely when you reach it.

Once data have been correctly identified and collected, data quality has to be taken into account; it cannot be taken for granted. This is another very common and costly mistake. Not all data values are accurate or valid. Analysis must take place to ensure that the data collected are correct and suitable for decision-making processes. The closer a data quality process can be inserted to the source, the better. Resolving data quality issues requires communication and working together with various groups and experts to resolve the root causes and underlying issues. By including a data stewardship function into the BICC, data quality topics can be adequately addressed.

Data storage is another consideration and obstacle to BI. Data often are stored in multiple formats, in multiple places, and in multiple databases. Data must be accessed and consolidated into consistent business views that support a fit-for-use approach for delivery despite storage complexities and limitations.

Technology Challenges. The proliferation of disconnected information silos poses another obstacle to the successful creation of knowledge within an organization. Since individual departments historically have been run like separate businesses, often each has been free to pursue its own IT infrastructure. This has resulted in the use of disparate hardware, platforms, systems standards, and databases throughout the organization—as well as often unfathomable difficulty in establishing and measuring progress toward enterprise-wide objectives. The BICC provides a means of addressing the whole information value chain—not just isolated parts of it—and enabling the business with the information it needs. Often the success of a particular piece of BI technology rests not only on its use in the organization but on what precedes it in the value chain.

Over time, organizations have accumulated a complex set of heterogeneous tools and infrastructure technologies that are not very well integrated. In some cases, a duplication of technologies used in various divisions of the same organization results in development and maintenance skills being thinly spread across all these different products. Therefore, the total cost of ownership (TCO) for managing this kind of complex environment is often much higher than it should be. Perhaps a bigger problem is that while this piecemeal approach has resulted in rapid deployment with good return on investment (ROI) in single business areas, the lack of coordination across projects has resulted in unintentional issues for the enterprise or the organization as a whole, making sharing information more difficult and incurring costs. The BICC plays a key role in balancing corporate governance while providing the flexibility required to get the job done.

Process Challenges. Business Intelligence is a process, not just a software product. No BI product, no matter how sophisticated or advanced, can address, fix, or replace processes alone. Process is a key to driving successful BI and successful organizations. Processes can be changed and measured and are documented, making them repeatable and able to adapt to changing business requirements. And the key to successful processes is people. Organizations that marry their human capital, culture, knowledge processes, and infrastructure by creating a BICC are most successful and are prepared and poised to meet the continuously changing demands of their customers and maximize potential.

Strategy Challenges. Aligning all BI initiatives in the organization so that they support the organizational strategy should be the goal. Yet often that goal is difficult to achieve—different groups in the organization have different BI needs and start their own independent BI projects. It is difficult to align all of them under a common BI strategy. Even if there is a strategy, often it is not executed effectively. Tasking a group of individuals (i.e., a

BICC) to define and subsequently support and monitor the success of the BI strategy is key. The BI strategy represents the way in which information delivery needs from management and operations are addressed and met.

Users Challenges. Business Intelligence can enhance everyone's decision making across the organization. Understanding the different audiences and their information needs, skills, and goals is vital for a successful BI implementation. A BICC can be instrumental in helping to identify the different audiences, understanding their needs, shaping their requirements and training, and coaching them so they can draw the right conclusion from the data available to them. The goal is to raise the overall maturity of the organization so it uses BI to its greatest effect.

Cultural Challenges. An organization's culture can be one of the single largest inhibitors to the successful use of BI. The culture needs to be such that it encourages fact-based decision making—that is, people can get to the information they need to make their decisions in an easy and timely fashion. Because every organization is unique, understanding its culture and how to best leverage it to the advantage of the organization is one of the contributions of the BICC. The BICC can help ensure that the strategic use of information becomes a core competency for the organization.

What Is a BICC?

As already described, a BICC is a cross-functional team with a permanent, formal organizational structure. It has defined tasks, roles, responsibilities, and processes for supporting and promoting the effective use of BI across an organization. It is staffed with employees from the organization itself, although some roles or functions might be outsourced. The BICC is tasked with driving the use of BI throughout the organization, making it available in the appropriate form to business users at different levels, and providing advice and support for all BI-related questions, including assistance with the interpretation of information.

A BICC enables the organization to coordinate and complement existing efforts in the area of BI, while reducing redundancy and increasing effectiveness. The centralization of these efforts ensures that information and best practices are communicated and shared through the entire organization so that everyone can benefit from successes and lessons learned.

A central mandate for the BICC is to enable knowledge transfer and enhance analytic skills and enable the business units to meet their goals. The BICC can coach and train business users to empower them with new skills that drive innovation and discovery. It can also be instrumental in turning analysis into action and ensuring greater information consumption and higher levels of ROI from BI.

Five Reasons to Establish a BICC

What are the arguments for establishing a BICC? A BICC can:

- Preserve and exploit the full value of technology investments.
- Integrate and consolidate business and analytical intelligence processes and initiatives.
- Reduce overall risk of implementation projects and project realization.
- Support business users in fully understanding data and acting properly on analyses.
- Ensure that BI knowledge (BI value, concepts, and technology) is shared throughout the organization.

Preserve and Exploit the Full Value of Technology Investments. Usually BI projects start out with great expectations for improvements to the business. However, whether these improvements can be achieved depends on many factors. It depends on how well the BI solution is understood, used, and supported in the organization. If the business users do not know how to use it, and if they are not able to get support when they have questions, then they will likely stop using the solution altogether or not use it to its full potential. One of the aims of the BICC is to provide the business with solutions that fit their requirements and support them in using them appropriately. The BICC is a group of BI experts who know the potential of BI and can make recommendations as to what to use, how, and why.

Integrate and Consolidate Business and Analytical Intelligence Processes and Initiatives. Often BI projects start in isolation. They are not in sync with other BI projects occurring elsewhere in the organization. Therefore, the result is a lot of overlap, redundancy, and information silos that do not allow the organization to connect different sources of information. What is worse, different solutions might provide inconsistent answers to the same question. This patchwork requires costly integration efforts. The BICC is an ideal instrument to oversee all BI-related initiatives at the enterprise level and can guard against this scenario. The BICC should be involved in defining the overall BI strategy so that the approach to BI shifts increasingly from tactical to strategic. It should evaluate which tools and technologies are fit for the purposes of the organization and drive standardization efforts that meets the needs of the business.

Reduce Overall Risk of Implementation Projects and Project Realization. Typical project risks include lack of the right project resources, lack of coordination, and prioritization between BI projects some of which might not fit into the overall BI architecture. The BICC should analyze and prioritize BI needs, design the overall BI architecture (and see to it that all projects fit with that architecture), and make sure that the organization makes best use of its BI skills and resources. Of equal importance is the consistency of definitions, processes, and methodologies to ensure smooth project implementations and repeatability.

Support Business Users in Fully Understanding Data and Acting Properly on Analyses. In many cases, business users need help with understanding what data are available to them for analysis, with recognizing which techniques to use for the analysis, or with understanding and acting properly on the information they are getting. An important part of the BICC's work is to provide BI training and coaching to business users to make sure they use BI technology effectively and efficiently.

Ensure that BI Knowledge (BI Value, Concepts, and Technology) Is Shared Throughout the Organization. An organization might not clearly see all the benefits it could gain from exploiting BI. The BICC would be instrumental in educating the organization about the value and the possibilities that BI delivers. This value is not restricted to the decision makers or the business analysts—many other business users can benefit from BI.

Today most organizations are tasked with doing more with fewer resources. A BICC provides an optimal solution for meeting the increasing demands of business users with fewer support staff and provides a forum for repeatable results, best practices, and collaboration across your organization. Thus, your successes can be documented, measured, and monitored for optimal performance. By streamlining operations, your organization can reduce overhead and information silos while increasing effectiveness. Business Intelligence that delivers context based on the past—as well as current and forecasted—information, coupled with the unique expertise and experience of your workforce, enables competitive differentiation.

What Gartner Says about BICCs

Gartner (www.gartner.com), a leading provider of research and analysis about the global IT industry, is a strong advocate of the concept of BICCs and has published numerous papers and research notes on the subject.

In his presentation "How to Organise for Success in BI," Bill Hostmann describes the mandate of a BICC: "The CC develops the overall strategic plan and priorities for BI, defines the requirements (including data quality and governance), and helps the organisation to interpret and apply the insight to business decisions."[1]

Gartner regards the existence of a BICC as instrumental for the success of a BI strategy. "Organizations that do not have a BICC should establish one, because it will increase the likelihood of success."[2]

One very obvious reason for setting up a BICC is the centralization of skills that might exist in different parts of the organization but that could be used more effectively and efficiently to increase the value of BI. The BICC should be the "center of gravitation," where different skill sets are combined for one common goal: to better understand the business and interpret current business results and to more accurately predict the future. In order to do this, a combination of business, IT, and analytical skills is required. (See Exhibit 1.1.)

Gartner points out that although there will be costs involved in the setup of a BICC (for staff, for creating standards and methodologies, for building skills, and for program management), those costs will be outweighed by the benefits organizations will obtain through BICCs, which include "higher levels of insight and impact, better use of skills and information, reduced costs, better data and increased agility."[3]

Gartner also stresses how important it is that the BICC work with a software vendor that understands the purpose and mandate of a BICC and is therefore able to form a positive relationship with it. Part of Gartner's

EXHIBIT 1.1   INTEGRATE ESSENTIAL BI COMPETENCIES

Integrate Essential BI Competencies and Skills with a BICC

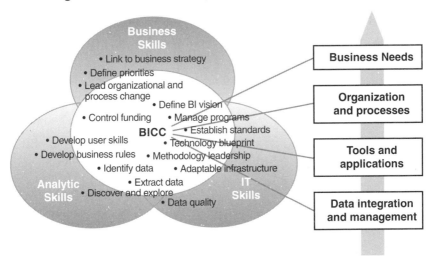

Source: Bill Hostmann, 'How to Organise for Success in BI,' Gartner Business Intelligence Summit, London, January 2005, 6.

BI vendor selection list is called "Issues to Focus on When Selecting a BI Vendor."[4]

SUMMARY

- A BICC can address a lot of issues—better use of BI across the organization, greater alignment and collaboration between business units,; a BI strategy that supports the corporate strategy; standardized BI processes and initiatives; consistency of definitions, processes, and methodologies; and higher ROI from BI.

- How does the BICC need to be set it up so that it can deliver on these promises? Obviously, it depends on many factors which will be explored in more depth throughout the book. However, three key elements will set the BICC off to a sound start.

    1. The BICC needs a clear mandate and strategy. It is not sufficient to say that the BICC is supposed to drive the BI strategy in the

organization if there is no clarity about what that strategy really is. Some time and effort needs to be invested in understanding the BI requirements of the organization in support of the corporate strategy.

2. If the organization is serious about this more strategic approach to BI, then the BICC needs support from very high up in the organization—ideally, executive sponsorship. Otherwise, it will not be visible and influential enough to play the crucial role that it should assume. The aim must be the alignment of BI goals across various functional areas, in support of the organization's strategy.

3. It is important to staff the BICC with representatives from both IT and the business. This combination ensures that both business understanding and IT know-how work in concert to address the business's BI requirements.

- Although a BICC is an excellent forum for addressing many tactical issues efficiently and effectively, it is imperative not to lose sight of the strategic value of a BICC. It is easy to be tactical. The results are easily quantifiable, and there is a never-ending list of problems to be solved and issues to tackle. Too often, however, organizations focus on the details and quickly lose sight of their vision.

- The BICC is the initial contact point in the organization for any questions or problems that relate to BI strategy or software. In cooperation with software vendors, the BICC provides optimal support for project teams, system administrators, and business users in the organization.

ENDNOTES

1. Bill Hostmann, "How to Organise for Success in BI," Gartner Business Intelligence Summit, London, January 2005, 6.
2. Alan Tiedrich, "The BI and Data Warehousing Tools Selection Process—A Recipe for Success," Gartner Business Intelligence Summit, London, January 2005, 8.
3. Ibid., 11.
4. Tiedrich, "The BI and Data Warehousing Tools Selection Process—A Recipe for Success."

CHAPTER 2

Business Intelligence in the Organization

OVERVIEW

How do other organizations plan for Business Intelligence? How do they ensure that the concept of BI is well embedded in the corporate structure and supported by the organization as a whole? How and by whom is BI used, driven, and supported? Do these organizations see value in setting up Business Intelligence Competency Centers?

To help you find answers to these questions, this chapter provides the results of a survey conducted by BetterManagement in 2005 entitled "How Do You Plan for Business Intelligence?" You can use the results as points of comparison for your own organization.

Background

In March 2005, BetterManagement subscribers completed a survey about the state of BI and BICCs in their organizations. This online survey was completed by 220 companies across various industries, sizes, geographic locations, and job levels. The specific objectives of the research were to determine how BICCs were developed and deployed within the organization.

Note: Some totals in the exhibits do not sum to 100% because of rounding.

Respondents

Industry. The participants in the study came from a variety of industries. The service industry had the highest representation with 18%, followed by information technology at 16%, banking and financial services at 10%, and manufacturing at 9%. Healthcare and government organizations accounted for 6% each, and pharma accounted for 5%. The remaining industries accounted for less than 5% each. (See Exhibit 2.27.)

Revenue. Just over four in ten of the companies that participated in the survey reported yearly revenue under $50 million. Another third (37%) were medium-size businesses of $50 million to under $1 billion, and the remainder, 19%, were enterprise-size organizations of $1 billion or more in revenue. (See Exhibit 2.28.)

Number of Employees. Corresponding to company revenue, 44% of the companies in the study had fewer than 250 employees. Organizations with

250 to under 10,000 workers accounted for an additional 42%, while the companies with 10,000 or more workers accounted for 14% of the total. (See Exhibit 2.29.)

Job Level. Nearly nine in ten (88%) of the respondents in the study were in management positions. Two-thirds (65%) were managers or directors and 23% were vice-presidents and C-level managers. (See Exhibit 2.30.)

Job Function. The respondents represented a variety of functions in the organization. Just over one in four (27%) were in general management. One in five (19%) were in information technology (IT) functions. One in ten (10%) performed marketing or operations functions. The remainder of the functional areas accounted for less than 10% of the total respondents. (See Exhibit 2.31.)

General Findings of the Survey

How Is Business Intelligence Used?

Slightly over eight in ten companies (84%) in the study reported that they use BI in their organizations. The results of the survey indicate that use of BI varies by geographic location and company size. Although there are not enough responses within each industry to provide statistical support, there appear to be differences by industry as well. Information technology organizations seem most likely to use BI, while insurance, manufacturing, and pharma companies appear to be least likely.

The results varied slightly by geographic location. Nine in ten (90%) North American companies currently use BI, versus eight in ten (around 80%) in the rest of the world. Seventy-one percent of companies in South America have BI functions. (See Exhibit 2.1.)

EXHIBIT 2.1   BI Usage by Geography

Total	84%
North America	90%
Asia Pacific	83%
Europe, Middle East, and Africa	81%
South America	71%

Not surprisingly, BI use is strongest among enterprise-size businesses of $1 billion or more in yearly revenue. Over nine in ten (93%) of the largest organizations reported using BI. There was no difference in the reported use of BI between small and medium-size organizations. (See Exhibit 2.2.)

What Is the Scope of BI Usage?

Among those companies that reported use of BI, the scope varies broadly. A strong percentage of firms use BI at the organizational (38%) or global (7%) level, but in other companies, the scope of BI is considerably narrower. Just over one in four (26%) respondents indicated use at the department level, with one in five (20%) using BI only at the individual level. These findings suggest that many deployments of BI are still siloed within specific areas of the company. (See Exhibit 2.3.)

The scope of usage of BI varies somewhat by company size, in interesting ways. Organizational or global use of BI is highest among enterprises of $1 billion or more (52%), higher than in small and midsize businesses. However, at least four in ten of the smaller and midsize businesses use BI at a global

EXHIBIT 2.2 BI USAGE BY COMPANY REVENUE	
Total	84%
Less than $50 million	82%
$50 to $999 million	81%
$1 billion or more	93%

EXHIBIT 2.3 "WHICH OF THE FOLLOWING BEST DESCRIBES THE SCOPE OF USAGE OF BI IN YOUR ORGANIZATION?"	
Used in my department, not sure about others	3%
On a regional level	4%
On a global level	7%
On an individual level	20%
On a department level	26%
On an organizational level	38%
Do not know	4%

or organizational level. This is likely due to the ease with which information can be shared due to proximity, fewer databases, and less complicated software in smaller organizations. Notably, individual use of BI declines with increased revenue. (See Exhibit 2.4.)

Who Uses the Results of BI?

The results of BI reach a broad spectrum of individuals in the company, but it appears that these results are focused primarily toward company management. In over half (58%) of the companies participating in the survey, BI results are used by top management. Department managers are the next most frequent users at 52%, followed by division heads at 41%. In just over a fourth (28%) of the companies, results are used corporate-wide at every level. This suggests that there is still significant room for the expansion of the BI footprint across levels of most organizations. The notion of "BI for the masses" has not yet been put into practice in a large number of companies. (See Exhibit 2.5.)

The survey indicates that as company revenue increases, so does the use of BI results across the organization. Small entities tend to use BI results primarily at the top management level (62%) and the department level (43%), and less so at the divisional level. These companies likely have a much

EXHIBIT 2.4   "WHICH OF THE FOLLOWING BEST DESCRIBES THE SCOPE OF USAGE OF BI IN YOUR ORGANIZATION?" (BY COMPANY SIZE)

	Total	Less than $50 million	$50–999 million	$1 billion or more
Used in my department, not sure about others	3%	3%	5%	0%
On a regional level	4%	4%	6%	0%
On a global level	7%	5%	8%	8%
On an individual level	20%	29%	14%	10%
On a department level	26%	14%	34%	36%
On an organizational level	38%	40%	32%	44%
Other	1%	3%	1%	0%
Do not know	3%	3%	0%	2%

EXHIBIT 2.5   "WHO USES THE RESULTS OF BI WITHIN YOUR ORGANIZATION?"

Top management	58%
Department managers	52%
Division heads	41%
Business analysts	29%
Used at every level	28%
Information consumers, end users	20%
Other	2%
Do not know	4%

flatter organization hierarchy. In midsize businesses, usage tends to be greatest among the department managers (62%), followed by top management (57%) and division heads (54%); again, use is fairly concentrated among management. However, larger organizations show a much higher level of BI penetration throughout all levels of the company, with strong usage among business analysts (46%) and end users (44%). (See Exhibit 2.6.)

How Are BI Needs Determined?

As further evidence of the siloed nature of the BI function in many organizations, nearly half (43%) of the companies surveyed indicated that each department or division establishes its own process to determine BI needs.

EXHIBIT 2.6   "WHO USES THE RESULTS OF BI WITHIN YOUR ORGANIZATION?" (BY COMPANY SIZE)

	Total	Less than $50 million	$50–999 million	$1 billion or more
Top management	58%	62%	57%	56%
Division heads	41%	23%	54%	51%
Department managers	52%	43%	62%	56%
Business analysts,	29%	17%	34%	46%
information consumers, end users	20%	12%	17%	44%
Used at every level	28%	27%	25%	31%
Other	1%	1%	1%	0%
Do not know	2%	2%	0%	2%

An additional 29% have no formal processes for doing so. Fewer than one in four (22%) of the companies with a BI function have a formal, standardized needs analysis process that spans the organization, significantly lower than the 38% (see Exhibit 2.3) that report using BI on an organizational level. (See Exhibit 2.7.)

The process for determining BI needs varies widely by company size. Small businesses showed no specific trend in this area. Four in ten (39%) small businesses indicated that they do not have a formal process to determine BI needs across the organization. However, 29% do have such a process, and in 26% of companies under $50 million in revenue, BI needs are determined at the department or division level.

As revenue increases, companies are more likely to determine BI needs by establishing processes at a department or division level. Interestingly, the larger a company, the less likely it is to have a formal needs analysis process that spans the organization. As the complexities of the business grow with company size, it appears that pockets of BI are used within the organization and managed independently. (See Exhibit 2.8.)

What Are the Characteristics of the BI Needs Analysis?

Among those companies that conduct a formal BI needs analysis, three-quarters (73%) perform an ongoing review of BI needs to ensure that new opportunities or requirements are identified and added to BI processes.

The primary components of a BI needs analysis are reports (73%) and strategic analytics (68%). Somewhat less frequently used in the analysis are compliance/corporate governance issues (46%) and early warning systems (44%). Fewer than one in three companies (29%) incorporate legal/regulatory reporting. (See Exhibit 2.9.)

EXHIBIT 2.7   "HOW ARE BI NEEDS DETERMINED?"

Formal standardized needs analysis process across the enterprise	22%
No formal needs analysis processes	29%
Each division/department establishes its own process	43%
Other	2%
Do not know	3%

EXHIBIT 2.8   "HOW ARE BI NEEDS DETERMINED?"
(BY COMPANY SIZE)

	Total	Less than $50 million	$50–999 million	$1 billion or more
Formal standardized needs analysis process across the enterprise	22%	29%	23%	8%
No formal needs analysis processes	29%	39%	25%	18%
Each division/department establishes its own process	43%	26%	48%	72%
Other	2%	4%	2%	0%
Do not know	3%	3%	3%	3%

EXHIBIT 2.9   "WHICH OF THE FOLLOWING DOES YOUR BI
NEEDS ANALYSIS INCLUDE?"

Report	73%
Strategic analytics (forecasting, modeling, etc.)	68%
Compliance/corporate governance	46%
Early warning/quality tracking	44%
Legal/regulatory reporting	29%

How Are BI Software Questions Requested and Received?

There appears to be no standard for requesting and receiving help with BI software questions, but the primary method used for dealing with these issues is through informal means within the organization. Four in ten (41%) of the companies surveyed indicated that they channel requests for help through internal "BI experts," who are not part of a formal BI structure. This indicates an immaturity in the use of BI, as companies have not yet dedicated resources to develop formal in-house experts as part of an overall program. In fact, only 17% indicated that help requests are sent through a BI support desk. (See Exhibit 2.10.)

EXHIBIT 2.10   "HOW DO USERS REQUEST AND RECEIVE HELP WHEN THEY HAVE QUESTIONS RELATED TO BI SOFTWARE?"

Requests are made informally to people known as experts in BI inside the organization	41%
Requests are channeled through an internal BI support desk	17%
Requests are channeled through the general internal support desk	25%
Requests are sent directly to a particular software vendor	8%
Other	11%
Do not know	13%

Although the most common method of dealing with requests for help concerning BI software is an informal use of internal "BI experts," the reliance on this method decreases among large enterprises. Dependence on a BI support desk increases significantly with company size, an indication that larger companies are more vested in BI and are spending resources to provide formal support. (See Exhibit 2.11.)

EXHIBIT 2.11   "HOW DO USERS REQUEST AND RECEIVE HELP WHEN THEY HAVE QUESTIONS RELATED TO BI SOFTWARE?" (BY COMPANY SIZE)

	Total	Less than $50 million	$50–999 million	$1 billion or more
Requests are made informally to people known as experts in BI inside the organization	41%	43%	46%	33%
Requests are channeled through an internal BI support desk	17%	10%	18%	31%
Requests are channeled through the general internal support desk	25%	25%	26%	26%
Requests are sent directly to a particular software vendor	8%	9%	6%	8%
Other	11%	9%	11%	10%
Do not know	13%	14%	11%	13%

How Effective Are BI Processes and Software?

In general, it appears that companies participating in this study are not completely satisfied with the effectiveness of their BI processes or software in providing users with the information they need to make effective decisions. Fewer than one in ten (9%) indicated that the BI processes or software are always effective, while only one in four (25%) reported that they are usually effective. This leaves six in ten (60%) with what appear to be hit-or-miss results from their BI software and an additional 6% who do not know how effective the BI software is. (See Exhibit 2.12.)

Organizations of $1 billion or more in revenue reported lower effectiveness of their BI software or processes in providing information for decision making than their smaller counterparts. None (0%) of the larger organizations indicated that the BI software always provides the needed information, and a larger percentage (18%) said that it rarely does. This result could be attributed to the increased complexity of the organization's information, the lack of maturity of the use of BI, or the software or processes themselves. (See Exhibit 2.13.)

Survey participants were asked to identify what three things BI users would benefit from most. The primary concern among those participating in the survey was the quality of information available (56%). This is consistent with other research that suggests that companies struggle with the basics of data quality and integrity. Another one in two companies (52%) indicated that users need access to information through easy-to-use interfaces. Supporting the notion that many companies are immature in their use of

EXHIBIT 2.12   "IN YOUR OPINION, HOW OFTEN DO THE BI PROCESSES AND/OR SOFTWARE USED IN YOUR ORGANIZATION PROVIDE USERS WITH ALL THE INFORMATION THEY NEED TO MAKE EFFECTIVE BUSINESS DECISIONS?"

Always	9%
Usually	25%
Sometimes	45%
Rarely	13%
Never	2%
Do not know	6%

EXHIBIT 2.13   "IN YOUR OPINION, HOW OFTEN DO THE BI
PROCESSES AND/OR SOFTWARE USED IN
YOUR ORGANIZATION PROVIDE USERS WITH
ALL THE INFORMATION THEY NEED TO MAKE
EFFECTIVE BUSINESS DECISIONS?"
(BY COMPANY SIZE)

	Total	Less than $50 million	$50–999 million	$1 billion or more
Always	9%	7%	15%	0%
Usually	25%	31%	15%	31%
Sometimes	45%	46%	48%	44%
Rarely	13%	10%	14%	18%
Never	2%	3%	2%	0%
Do not know	6%	4%	6%	8%

BI, four in ten companies reported that users need help with interpretation (44%) and gaining access to the appropriate information (41%).

Mentioned less often were training in the use of BI tools (21%) and a formal assessment of information needs (27%). This result could indicate that companies first need to resolve the issues of data quality, reporting, and interpretation before they conduct formal assessments and BI training. (See Exhibit 2.14.)

The most important enhancement users would benefit from in large companies is access to relevant information in easy-to-use reporting interfaces (67%). Given that the footprint of BI use is broader across the organization

EXHIBIT 2.14   "IN YOUR OPINION, WHICH THREE OF THE
FOLLOWING WOULD BI USERS BENEFIT
FROM MOST?"

Improved quality of information available to them	56%
Access to relevant information in easy-to-use reporting interfaces for ad hoc reporting	52%
Assistance with interpreting and drawing conclusions from the information	44%
Access to relevant information in standard reports	41%
An overview of which data is available for analysis	35%
A formal assessment of their information needs	27%
Training in use of BI tools	21%

in large businesses, it follows that ease of information access and reporting are of highest interest. These larger companies are less concerned than their smaller counterparts about assistance with interpretation and in help gaining access to relevant information in standard reports. These activities are likely already in place in enterprise-size entities.

In small organizations, the respondents indicated less concern about users getting an overview of the data available for analysis. Again, a smaller business would have fewer databases and less disparate information across the company; therefore, perhaps the small business would have a better general understanding of the information available. (See Exhibit 2.15.)

EXHIBIT 2.15 "IN YOUR OPINION, WHICH THREE OF THE FOLLOWING WOULD BI USERS BENEFIT FROM MOST?" (BY COMPANY SIZE)

	Total	Less than $50 million	$50–999 million	$1 billion or more
Improved quality of information available to them	56%	56%	57%	56%
Access to relevant information in easy-to-use reporting interfaces for ad hoc reporting	52%	49%	48%	67%
Assistance with interpreting and drawing conclusions from the information	44%	51%	49%	28%
Access to relevant information in standard reports	41%	48%	42%	31%
An overview of which data is available for analysis	35%	27%	40%	41%
A formal assessment of their information needs	27%	26%	28%	23%
Training in use of BI tools	21%	21%	20%	23%

BUSINESS INTELLIGENCE COMPETENCY CENTERS

Presence of BICCs

Business Intelligence Competency Centers are present in just under one in four (23%) of the companies surveyed, with an additional 9% planning to implement one in the next 12 months and 21% more considering implementing one. Over four in ten (44%) of the companies do not currently have plans for a competency center. (See Exhibit 2.16.)

The absolute number of companies that report having BICCs in this survey is 42; therefore, the information in the sections that follow should be viewed as directional and not statistically significant.

Business Intelligence Competency Centers used by the respondents in this study appear to be fairly well established, with nearly eight in ten centers at least a year old. Only one in five (19%) established a BICC in the last year. Nearly half (48%) have had a center for more than two years. (See Exhibit 2.17.)

EXHIBIT 2.16 "DO YOU CURRENTLY HAVE A BICC IN YOUR ORGANIZATION?"

Currently have	23%
Planned in next 12 months	9%
Considering	21%
Not planned	44%
Do not know	4%

EXHIBIT 2.17 "HOW LONG HAS YOUR COMPANY HAD A BICC?"

Less than a year	19%
1 to 2 years	31%
More than 2 years	48%
Do not know	2%

BICC Size and Support

The majority of BICCs are small, with ten or fewer employees (79%). Although most centers support fewer than 500 users, there seems to be an imbalance at the top end. Only 15% of the companies with a BICC report employing more than ten staff members in the BICC, while 29% have 1,000 or more BI users. (See Exhibits 2.18 and 2.19.)

BICC Funding

The majority of the companies reporting that they have BICCs indicated that the center is a cost center (64%). Only one in five (21%) companies uses a chargeback to the functional departments. (See Exhibit 2.20.)

EXHIBIT 2.18   "CURRENTLY, HOW MANY STAFF ARE IN THE BICC?"

Fewer than 5	55%
5 to 10	24%
11 to 20	5%
More than 20	10%
Do not know	7%

EXHIBIT 2.19   "HOW MANY BUSINESS USERS DOES THE BICC SUPPORT?"

Fewer than 500	60%
500 to 999	12%
1,000 to 2,000	15%
More than 2,000	14%

EXHIBIT 2.20   "HOW DOES YOUR COMPANY FUND THE BICC?"

It charges the functional department for its services	21%
It is a cost center	64%
Other	5%
Do not know	10%

BICC Organizational Fit

Again, the actual number of BICCs evaluated in this research is 42. Among those, more than a third (36%) report directly into business management. A nearly equal portion, 38%, are part of the IT division. In a few cases, the competency centers report to marketing or are virtual centers (10% each). In two instances (5%), the centers report to the finance division. (See Exhibit 2.21.)

Benefits and Disadvantages of a BICC

The primary advantage of BICCs cited by the participants in this research is the increased usage of BI in the organization (74%). Other benefits reported among just under half of the respondents include increased business user satisfaction with BI, better understanding of the value of BI, and increased decision-making speed. Decreased costs, both staff and software, were noted by about one in four. (See Exhibit 2.22.)

EXHIBIT 2.21   "WHERE DOES THE BICC FIT IN THE STRUCTURE OF YOUR COMPANY'S ORGANIZATION?"

Reports to business management	36%
Part of the IT division	38%
Part of the finance division	5%
Part of the marketing division	10%
It is a virtual BICC (without solid reporting lines)	10%
Do not know	2%

EXHIBIT 2.22   "WHAT BENEFITS, IF ANY, HAS YOUR COMPANY GAINED FROM THE BICC?"

Increased usage of BI	74%
Increased business user satisfaction	48%
Increased decision-making speed	45%
Better understanding of the value of BI	45%
New ways of applying BI	36%
Decreased staff costs	26%
Decreased software costs	24%
Other	7%
Do not know	5%

Approximately a third of the participants (36%) indicated that they have experienced no disadvantages to the BICC. Three in ten (31%) are concerned about overlapping and unclear responsibilities. Several (17%) view the competency center as a bottleneck. A few individuals indicated that they see no tangible improvements to business users and that support for the center is not timely. (See Exhibit 2.23.)

Potential Responsibilities for the BICC

Respondents were asked what functional areas they think should be in the scope of the BICC. Over three-quarters (76%) indicated that knowledge management should fall under the competency center. Approximately seven in ten indicated that business-related consulting (71%) and analytics (67%) should be included. Data warehousing and enterprise data model management were mentioned by 62% of the respondents. Training was noted by just over one half (55%). (See Exhibit 2.24.)

Decision Factors in Establishing a BICC

The most important factor in the decision to establish a BICC was to drive the use of BI to different levels of the organization. This factor indicates an interest in further developing the use of information and becoming more advanced in how information is used across the organization. Two other key factors were related to dealing with integration issues and supporting a particular solution. Interestingly, managing cost and lowering the total cost of ownership were not rated as high as most other factors. (See Exhibit 2.25.)

EXHIBIT 2.23 "WHAT DISADVANTAGES, IF ANY, HAS YOUR COMPANY EXPERIENCED AS A RESULT OF THE BICC?"

No disadvantages	36%
Overlapping and unclear responsibilities	31%
The competency center is perceived as a bottleneck	17%
No tangible improvements to business users	12%
Support is not timely	12%
Other	10%

EXHIBIT 2.24 "WHAT FUNCTIONAL AREAS DO YOU THINK SHOULD BE THE RESPONSIBILITY OF A BICC?"

Knowledge management	76%
Business-related consulting	71%
Analytics	67%
Data warehousing	62%
Enterprise data model management	62%
Training	55%
Help desk	41%
Integration process management	41%
Technical consulting	36%
Contracts management	33%
Systems management	31%
Other	5%
Do not know	2%

EXHIBIT 2.25 "ON A SCALE FROM 1 TO 5 (WITH 1 BEING 'NOT AT ALL IMPORTANT' AND 5 BEING 'EXTREMELY IMPORTANT') PLEASE RATE THE FOLLOWING FACTORS IN YOUR DECISION TO SET UP A BICC"

	Average rating
Drives the use of BI to different levels of the organization	4.1
Deals with integration issues	3.9
Supports particular solution(s)	3.9
Addresses lack of resources and skills	3.6
Optimizes the use of human resources through shared services	3.6
Manages costs and lowers total cost of ownership	3.3
Focuses on compliance issues	3.1
Manages merger/acquisition projects	2.5

Metrics for Success of BICCs

The success of BICCs is measured primarily through business user satisfaction (67%). With driving BI to different levels of the organization the main factor for establishing the BICC, it could be that the centers are interested in ensuring that BI is meeting the users' needs. Other key metrics for the success of BICCs include the availability of information and the accuracy and reliability of that information. As previously indicated, data quality is a chief concern among BI users (see Exhibit 2.15). A small number (12%) have not measured the success of the competency center. (See Exhibit 2.26.)

Additional Findings

Exhibits 2.27 through 2.31 provide some additional information about the respondents to the BetterManagement survey in terms of their industry, revenue/turnover, number of employees, job level, and function.

EXHIBIT 2.26   "WHICH OF THE FOLLOWING METRICS DO YOU USE TO MEASURE THE SUCCESS OF YOUR COMPETENCY CENTER?"

Business user satisfaction	67%
Availability of information	60%
Accuracy and reliability of information	57%
Staff costs	41%
Decision-making speed	38%
Software costs	36%
We have not measured the success of the competency center	12%
Other	7%
Do not know	2%

EXHIBIT 2.27   "WHICH OF THE FOLLOWING CATEGORIES BEST DESCRIBES YOUR ORGANIZATION'S INDUSTRY?"

Services	18%
Information technology	16%
Banking and financial services	10%
Manufacturing	9%
Healthcare	6%
Government	6%
Pharma	5%
Telecommunications and media	4%
Insurance	3%
Trade	3%
Utilities	2%
Oil, gas, and mining	1%
Other	19%

EXHIBIT 2.28 "WHAT IS THE APPROXIMATE ANNUAL
REVENUE/TURNOVER OF YOUR
ORGANIZATION IN U.S. DOLLARS?"

Less than $50 million	44%
$50 to $99 million	9%
$100 to $249 million	10%
$250 to $499 million	7%
$500 to $749 million	5%
$750 million to $999 million	6%
$1 billion or more	19%

EXHIBIT 2.29 "HOW MANY EMPLOYEES ARE THERE IN ALL
LOCATIONS OF YOUR COMPANY?"

Fewer than 250	44%
250 to 999	12%
1,000 to 4,999	19%
5,000 to 7,499	7%
7,500 to 9,999	4%
10,000 or more	14%

EXHIBIT 2.30 "WHICH OF THE FOLLOWING MOST CLOSELY
DESCRIBES YOUR JOB LEVEL?"

Manager	37%
Director	28%
C-level, president, etc.	14%
Vice-president	9%
Nonmanager/analyst/professional	9%
Other	3%

EXHIBIT 2.31 "WHICH OF THE FOLLOWING MOST CLOSELY
DESCRIBES YOUR JOB FUNCTION?"

General management	27%
Information technology	19%
Operations	10%
Marketing	10%
Finance	7%
Sales	6%
Human resources	6%
Other	16%

Summary

- The survey shows that BI usage still seems to be restricted to management level in most companies. In addition, the survey results show that a majority of individuals are not satisfied with the results they are currently getting out of BI. Looking at the "wish list" from the business users shown in Exhibit 2.15, it seems that users still lack trust in the quality of information and need easy-to-use interfaces and support with interpreting information.

- These results indicate that there is room for BI to improve in both quantity (BI must reach out to more users) and quality.

- Only rarely is there a cross-organizational BI needs analysis process or dedicated resources to support BI usage in organizations. As a result, there seems to be a lack of infrastructure both on the needs analysis and the support side.

- Just over 20% of the respondents indicate that they have put a BICC in place. Another 30% are thinking about implementing one. Obviously more and more organizations are exploring the concept.

- A large number of those organizations that have a BICC report that they see an increase in BI usage, higher business-user satisfaction, and increased decision-making speed. This perception could indicate that organizations that have BICCs are successful in getting more value out of their BI investment, which in turn means that they are able to address their number-one reason for establishing BICCs: to drive the use of BI to different levels of the organization.

- Many BICCs are measured by business users' satisfaction and by the availability and reliability of information to ensure that they deliver ongoing value to their constituents.

CHAPTER 3

Primary Functions of the Business Intelligence Competency Center

Overview

The Business Intelligence Competency Center operates as a support and service center for the business units in the organization, potentially spanning multiple divisions and geographical boundaries. A clear definition of the BICC's responsibilities and agreement about its functions are vital. You need that clarity in order to manage the expectations for the BICC and to keep it working efficiently, given various service requests and support queries.

The BICC needs to be supported by an infrastructure that helps it to manage and prioritize the workload while keeping the work transparent and predictable for its internal customers. You will need to define both service levels and support infrastructure for the relationships that the BICC has with the internal business units and with software vendors. Which functional areas should the BICC consist of? (See Exhibit 3.1.)

EXHIBIT 3.1   FUNCTIONAL AREAS IN THE BICC

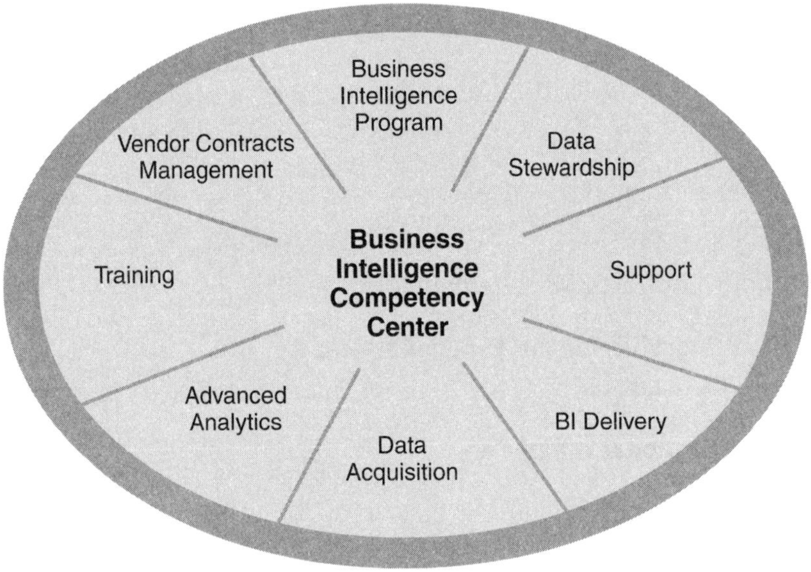

Functional Areas Inside the BICC

The functional areas shown in Exhibit 3.1 are important to cover in a BICC. Your organization might decide that only some of those areas should be included in your BICC. For example, your current organizational structure might require you to centralize only some of those functions in your BICC, while others would remain in other functional units. However, we believe that the described functions must be covered by your organization in some form—in the BICC itself, in the information technology (IT) department, in the business units, or outsourced to an external provider.

The functions that should be covered in the BICC include:

- Business Intelligence Program
- Data stewardship
- Support
- BI delivery
- Data acquisition
- Advanced analytics
- Training
- Vendor contracts management

Business Intelligence Program

The Business Intelligence Program function is the cornerstone of the BICC. It oversees and coordinates all of the activities of the BICC and is the interface to the business units. Specifically, the Business Intelligence Program function is involved in defining the Business Intelligence (BI) objectives and strategy and tracks the success of that strategy over time. It ensures that the BI strategy is executed, enables the business needs and that it supports the organization's overall strategy.

Here, business users can get advice and coaching on how to use BI analyses and interpret the results. The BI Program function also acts as the project office for all BI-related projects. It keeps the organization abreast of new BI trends and technologies and explains how the organization could benefit from them. Furthermore, it is responsible for sharing BI knowledge throughout the organization.

Data Stewardship

The data stewardship function takes care of administering technical metadata and ensures its alignment with business metadata. It is responsible for data standards, data quality, and data governance.

Support

The support function acts as the second-level support for BI problems. The assumption is that first-level support would be handled by the general service desk in the organization. The BICC support function clarifies the BI problem messages, analyses the problem in detail, and gets back to the user with the solution. In case the problem cannot be solved in-house, it will be passed to the software vendor.

BI Delivery

The BI delivery function takes care of the applications for delivery and distribution of information throughout the entire life cycle of the applications, including their design, development, testing, and maintenance. These applications comprise reporting, business logic, and portals—that is, all applications that transform the data residing in data warehouses or other BI storage areas into BI.

Data Acquisition

The data acquisition function handles the back-end–related BI activities. It takes care of data integration and data store development, testing, and maintenance as well as the overall warehouse design and integration projects.

Advanced Analytics

The advanced analytics function specializes in statistical analysis, modeling, optimization techniques, forecasting, and data mining. It handles complex analytical requests coming from the business units.

Training

The training function trains business users in BI concepts and BI applications. It coaches them by providing answers to their BI questions. It also takes care of any BI product-specific training and certifications for project teams or business users.

Vendor Contracts Management

The vendor contracts management function handles all the license- and contract-related issues, such as user licenses, software distribution, and service-level agreements with BI vendors and product evaluations. This function also acts as an interface to the organization's purchasing and legal departments.

A fundamental decision you will have to make is which functional areas you would like your BICC to cover. Consider these questions:

- What are the goals and objectives of your BI strategy?
- Based on that strategy, which deliverables, services, and support to the business and to IT will need to be provided?
- As a consequence, which of the suggested functional areas should be covered and how?
- Who is going to deliver the services?
  - BICC
  - IT department
  - Business units
  - External provider (e.g., software vendor)
- What individuals in the organization will be asking for the services (e.g., executives, business users, IT), and what is their user profile?
- What will be the nature, complexity, frequency, importance, and timing of the services?
- Based on the answers to the previous questions, what are the goals and objectives for the BICC? How, as a consequence, should the BICC be staffed?
- What are the processes and internal service-level agreements for making, working on, and responding to service requests?
- What organizational changes will occur as a result of the answers to the previous questions, and how should they be addressed?

Sometimes service requests cannot be taken care of by only one specific function in the BICC; in such cases, several functions must cooperate in order to address the service request. It is also possible that the same person might take over several roles (e.g., working as an application developer in projects, but also providing second-level support). Therefore, it is important to understand that the functions described in the next section do not necessarily correspond to real-world teams or departments. The functions constitute a purely theoretical bundling of tasks and do not necessarily correspond to how the BICC should be structured organizationally. Besides, you could choose to outsource one or several of these functions to an external provider.

However, our recommendation is that any function that requires profound business understanding (e.g., the BI Program function) should *not* be outsourced. For competitive and intellectual ownership reasons, it is important that functions critical to realizing a business strategy be owned and driven from within the organization.

We believe the BI Program, data stewardship, and support functions to be the most essential, and therefore the minimum, functions necessary in a BICC. Data standards, quality, and governance are absolute musts for getting value out of BI. Supporting and enabling the business users is one of the main motivations for establishing a BICC. However, the BI Program function is what makes a competency center a true *Business Intelligence* Competency Center because it is the BI Program that maintains the business alignment and carries the BICC's strategic focus and mandate.

What functions will your BICC address? The next section provides a checklist that contains more details on the individual functions.

DETAILED CHECKLIST FOR THE FUNCTIONAL AREAS IN THE BICC

This checklist provides more detail on what should be covered as part of the functional areas. It can be used to decide which functional areas, and which topics within those areas, should be within the BICC's responsibility, which ones would not be covered at all, and which ones would be looked after elsewhere. An electronic version of this checklist can be downloaded from the BICC book Web site (see the Preface of this book for details).

Functional Area	Covered by the BICC	Not Covered at All	Function Covered Outside of the BICC by . . .
Business Intelligence Program	☐	☐	
Defining the BI and AI (analytical intelligence) strategy and its link to the corporate strategy	☐	☐	
Managing standards and templates for BI/analytical intelligence	☐	☐	
Establishing and monitoring key performance indicators (KPIs) (e.g., return on investment [ROI]) for the success of the BI strategy and the BICC	☐	☐	
Business-related consulting	☐	☐	
BI project office management	☐	☐	
Function specialization[1]	☐	☐	
Service management	☐	☐	
Internal marketing of the BICC[2]	☐	☐	
Knowledge management[3]	☐	☐	
Metadata management[4]	☐	☐	
BI-related security (common to all functional areas)	☐	☐	
Information quality	☐	☐	

[1]If the focus of the BICC is on a particular topic (i.e., customer relationship management, compliance, etc.), a business specialist for this topic should be working with the BICC. This individual would act as a business advisor for this topic to the BICC.

[2]This includes keeping the organization informed about the BICC's service offering to the business. It should also take care of informing the rest of the organization about the status of BI projects, plans for the future, and in general market the BICC as a center of expertise for BI-related questions.

[3]See the section entitled "Knowledge Management" in Chapter 7 for more information about the importance of knowledge management in the BICC context.

[4]For corporate BI metadata in general, and specifically for business metadata.

(continues)

Functional Area	Covered by the BICC	Not Covered at All	Function Covered Outside of the BICC by . . .
Service-level agreements (between the BICC and the business units)	☐	☐	
Cooperation with corporate IT with regard to hardware architecture, capacity planning, etc.	☐	☐	
Data Stewardship	☐	☐	
Metadata management ownership (technical metadata only)	☐	☐	
Data standards	☐	☐	
Definitions	☐	☐	
Data governance	☐	☐	
Data quality	☐	☐	
Support	☐	☐	
Second-level support[5]	☐	☐	
User management	☐	☐	
BI Delivery	☐	☐	
Front-end BI distribution (portal, channel delivery, etc.)	☐	☐	
Front-end BI application development, warehouse-based applications (reporting, OLAP [Online Analytical Processing], etc.)	☐	☐	
Testing	☐	☐	
Maintenance	☐	☐	
Technical consulting	☐	☐	
Data Acquisition	☐	☐	
Data integration/development/ testing/maintenance	☐	☐	
Data store development/ optimization/testing/ maintenance	☐	☐	

[5]We recommend that first-level technical support be handled by the general service desk in your organization.

Functional Area	Covered by the BICC	Not Covered at All	Function Covered Outside of the BICC by . . .
Scheduling	☐	☐	
Technical consulting	☐	☐	
Integration processes	☐	☐	
Advanced Analytics	☐	☐	
Statistical analyses, modeling, forecasting, optimization, etc.	☐	☐	
Data mining	☐	☐	
Research and experimenting	☐	☐	
Data preparation for analytical purposes	☐	☐	
Training	☐	☐	
Training development	☐	☐	
Training (business use)	☐	☐	
Training (product-specific)	☐	☐	
Vendor contracts management	☐	☐	
User licenses	☐	☐	
Service-level agreements with vendors (BI related)	☐	☐	
Vendor management	☐	☐	
Product evaluation	☐	☐	
Interface to purchasing/legal departments	☐	☐	

Related Functional Areas

The next functions should probably *not* form part of the BICC. They are functions that are not strictly BI related and will exist for other purposes in the organization. However, they are listed here for completeness. It is important that these functions work closely with the BICC.

Functional Area	Covered by the BICC	Not Covered at All	Function Covered Outside of the BICC by . . .
Service Desk/Support	☐	☐	

Note: The assumption is that user calls are first routed to the general service desk and then are dispatched to the BICC.

Check messages for completeness	☐	☐	
Log/classify requests	☐	☐	
Dispatch problem message to the appropriate support organization	☐	☐	
Track requests and provide ongoing service to the user while the problem is being worked on	☐	☐	
Escalate	☐	☐	
System Administration	☐	☐	
Services management	☐	☐	
Service-level agreements	☐	☐	
New software versions	☐	☐	
Hot fixes	☐	☐	
Infrastructure support	☐	☐	
Infrastructure administration	☐	☐	
Technical Change Management	☐	☐	
Moving to production	☐	☐	
Testing management	☐	☐	
Move management	☐	☐	
Database Administration	☐	☐	
Log/classify requests	☐	☐	
Track requests	☐	☐	
Escalate	☐	☐	

Summary

- The functional area descriptions and checklists provided in this chapter can be used to stimulate discussion about what the BICC's responsibilities should include.

- Although it is important to look at the big picture of BI and include all relevant aspects in the discussion, this does not necessarily mean that the BICC must cover all of the functions by itself.

- In some cases, it might make sense to leave some BI responsibility in the business units. However, roles and responsibilities need to be defined clearly, and processes must be developed to ensure smooth cooperation.

- When the functional areas have been defined, the next step is to decide how to staff them (Chapter 5), how they would be working (Chapter 6), how to address cultural aspects that come up as a result of the BICC setup (Chapter 7), and which technology is required for the BICC to best support its user community (Chapter 8).

CHAPTER 4

Planning a Business Intelligence Competency Center: Using the Information Evolution Model

OVERVIEW

In Chapter 1, we talked about the Business Intelligence strategy that the Business Intelligence Competency Center should drive forward. However, for the BICC to do that, first the strategy has to be identified and planned.

It makes sense to start with an analysis of the current and future BI requirements in the organization. This analysis should not focus on systems and technology alone. It should also examine the people using the information, the processes that support them, and the "information culture" in the organization.

A comprehensive BI strategy assessment is a must before a BICC can be established. Such an assessment will provide the BICC with a "legitimized" mandate that comes from the individuals it intends to serve—the business users. Involving the business will also greatly facilitate buy-in for the BICC when it is up and running.

Instead of restricting the analysis to the management level, obtain a view from various levels in the organization, as well as from the various business functions, to examine how information currently is used and where improvement is necessary. Taking this step will give you a comprehensive inventory of shortcomings that obviously need to be evaluated and prioritized.

Note: The BI requirements of an organization are subject to constant change. The changes are driven largely by fluctuating business requirements. Therefore, an organization must conduct periodic analyses of its BI requirements.

After analyzing companies of all sizes across a broad range of industries, SAS developed the Information Evolution Model.[1] The model describes the way in which organizations use information to advance the business.

The model can help you to identify and measure your organization's current level of BI maturity. From there you can define the necessary steps to align your BI and business strategy to support your future short- and long-term business objectives. The model consists of four critical dimensions as well as of five levels of BI maturity.

Using this model offers your organization these advantages:

- You obtain a description of how enterprise-wide intelligence enables better decision making to keep up with the competition or gain a competitive edge in the marketplace.

- The model provides you with the basis for setting a vision to reach BI goals, including a road map for the implementation of solutions to support those goals.
- You get a framework for describing your current BI environment as well as for articulating future BI goals as part of an intelligent enterprise.
- The model assists you in establishing a process for understanding and changing how information is used throughout the organization.
- It helps you to pull together all the information relevant for your business metrics or key performance indicators (KPIs) for improved decision making.

To start, let us look first at the four dimensions of the Information Evolution Model.

FOUR CRITICAL DIMENSIONS OF THE INFORMATION EVOLUTION MODEL

Technology alone does not solve business problems or provide useful, timely information to the right people so they can make better decisions. Rather, the interaction of four critical business dimensions is what solves problems. (See Exhibit 4.1.)

What are these dimensions and what do they contribute to your organization's ability to leverage information?

Dimension 1: Human Capital (People)

Human capital consists of the information skills of individuals within the organization and the quantifiable aspects of their capabilities, recruitment, training, assessment, and alignment toward enterprise goals.

The human capital dimension asks these questions: Who is involved in using information throughout the organization, and are they using the information to its best potential? This dimension includes critical thinking skills, commitment to fact-based decisions, ongoing training, and the improvement of information skills. This dimension also holds that management is accountable for supporting and driving the use of information in the organization. People are encouraged to work in dynamic, often virtual, implementation teams.

FOUR DIMENSIONS OF THE INFORMATION EVOLUTION MODEL

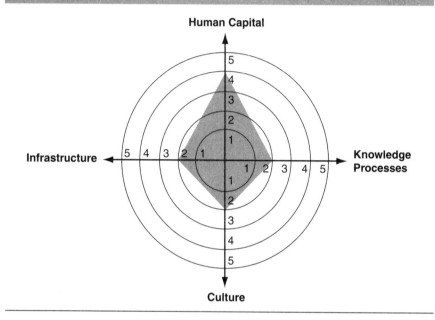

The human capital dimension includes these elements:

- Skills
- Training
- Alignment of individual and enterprise goals
- Individual performance evaluation

Dimension 2: Knowledge Processes

This dimension looks at which information-related activities must be performed. It describes the information processes in place to improve information flow and use, including governance and how the use of information is tied to performance goals with a reward system. It also describes how the organization supports its commitment to the strategic use of information in its business processes. Information access needs to be provided and strategic feedback given on the use of information.

The knowledge processes dimension includes these elements:

- Role of information in decision making
- Role of information in corporate knowledge sharing
- Improving information accuracy and quality

Dimension 3: Culture

Culture refers to the organizational and human influences on information flow. That is, culture includes the moral, social, and behavioral norms of the organization as shown in the attitudes, beliefs, and priorities of its members, and as related to the use and value of information as a long-term strategic corporate asset.

The characteristics of a fact-based decision culture include:

- Results- and outcome-focused behavior
- Monitoring and swiftly responding to environmental changes
- Aggressive, innovative risk seeking
- Rewarding and recognizing the use of information for decision making
- Creating an integrated, coordinated, collaborative, and interdependent work environment

The culture dimension includes these elements:

- Level of cooperation
- Responsiveness to change
- Individual empowerment
- Continuous business improvement
- Management style
- Relationship with customers
- Corporate performance evaluation
- Risk tolerance

Dimension 4: Infrastructure

Infrastructure includes the hardware, software, networking tools, and technologies that create, manage, store, disseminate, and apply information.

What are the information-related technologies and tools? Which standards and policies need to be implemented? This dimension encompasses the tools and technologies as well as the related standards, policies, and best practices to support the use of information for decision making. It also includes the hardware and software infrastructure and whether that infrastructure is agile, stable, scalable, and integrated in order to fully leverage technology. It further covers monitoring and enforcing data quality and common definitions for metadata.

The infrastructure dimension includes these elements:

- Hardware and software
- Capture of business and technical metadata
- Integration of data sources
- Maturity of intelligence architecture

Note: These four critical business dimensions need to move cooperatively to be effective. If there is any significant difference in the level of maturity shown by the human capital, knowledge processes, culture, and infrastructure dimensions of the business, organizational tension will be evident and will hamper the performance and use of information.

FIVE LEVELS OF MATURITY IN THE INFORMATION EVOLUTION MODEL

Organizations tend to follow a certain pattern regarding the use of information. The Information Evolution Model describes this development.[2] Understanding the model not only helps you see where you currently are in the process of information "evolution," but also helps you plan how to move to a higher level.

You will notice in the descriptions that follow that the levels build on each other. (See Exhibit 4.2.) In many organizations, there will be groups that operate on different levels, although the overall rating of an organization defaults to the lowest common denominator.

Level 1: Operate

The "operate" level represents the initial level of information evolution, typical of start-up, struggling, or entrepreneurial organizations. The focus

EXHIBIT 4.2   FIVE LEVELS OF THE INFORMATION
EVOLUTION MODEL

The Information Evolution Model

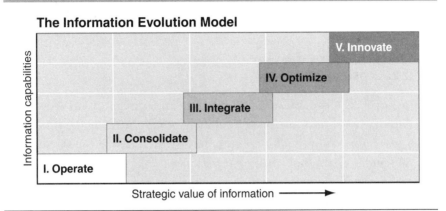

is on the here and now, as businesses emphasize activities required to support the day-to-day operations. Organizations at Level 1 are successful due to visionary leaders, mavericks, and luck.

At this level, information equals personal power, and everyone has their own version of the truth. These organizations generally operate and make decisions in an unplanned and chaotic information environment. They do not have long-range plans or information standards, and information provides little or no benefit to the organization. (See Exhibit 4.3.)

Level 1 indicators include:

- Individuals have authority over information usage.

- Information infrastructure (technology and governance processes) is nonexistent, limited, highly variable, or subjective.

EXHIBIT 4.3   FIRST LEVEL OF THE INFORMATION
EVOLUTION MODEL

Level 1	Human Capital	Knowledge Processes	Culture	Infrastructure
OPERATE	Individual	Personal	Me	Manual systems of nonnetworked PCs

- Individual methods of finding and analyzing information are used. Little is documented, and process repeatability is limited to individual knowledge. There is little or no transparency.

- Individual results are adopted as "corporate truth" without due diligence.

Level 2: Consolidate

At this level, the organization has progressed to departmental or functional focal points. Information is combined into departmental or functional databases. Information within a unit is consistent and governed by departmental standards and tools. An organization at Level 2 uses information to achieve localized goals and objectives. Enterprise goals and objectives often are tracked only manually, and in many cases, enterprise goals are secondary to departmental goals.

Data stores and decisional applications are designed, developed, and supported from a departmental perspective, without a large degree of consideration for the organization as a whole. Information silos result in little control over information at the organizational level.

More organizations will perceive themselves to be in Level 2 than in Level 1. However, within the context of the Information Evolution Model, Level 2 is a stepping-stone to the enterprise integration achieved in Level 3. (See Exhibit 4.4.)

Level 2 indicators include:

- Decisions are based on departmental orientation.

- Independent department islands of information are created.

- Data are consolidated and accessed at the departmental level.

EXHIBIT 4.4   SECOND LEVEL OF THE INFORMATION EVOLUTION MODEL

Level 2	Human Capital	Knowledge Processes	Culture	Infrastructure
CONSOLIDATE	Functional group	Department	Our group versus the rest of the organization	Functional systems

- Departmental business measures are inconsistent across the enterprise.
- Multiple interfaces and data extracts from operational databases reflect different versions of the truth.

Level 3: Integrate

At the third level, silos of information are integrated into an enterprise-wide view. The organization establishes an integrated information environment. It recognizes the importance of defining data and information consistently across the enterprise. This means one version of the truth is agreed on and an informed view of operations is available.

Enterprise-wide access to information is uniform and widespread, and information processes are repeatable. Most crucial to this level is that information needs and requirements can be traced clearly to organizational objectives. As a result, information projects have higher success rates. Companies at Level 3 gain awareness of what information can do for them. (See Exhibit 4.5.)

Level 3 indicators include:

- Cross-enterprise information access is in place.
- Decision making is in an enterprise-wide context.
- An enterprise information governance process is in place.
- Enterprise data frameworks are in place.
- Information management concepts are applied and accepted.
- Institutional awareness of data quality is valued. Data quality feedback is established.

EXHIBIT 4.5 THIRD LEVEL OF THE INFORMATION EVOLUTION MODEL

Level 3	Human Capital	Knowledge Processes	Culture	Infrastructure
INTEGRATE	Enterprise group	Enterprise	All of us	Enterprise systems

Level 4: Optimize

At this level, the organization has the ability to monitor the marketplace and realign itself quickly to meet market demands. Information is integral to measuring, aligning, and improving business processes, and information drives fact-based decision making. The environment is typified by an enterprise focus on process optimization and process extension. Most important, the environment is improved by an understanding of, and alignment with, the needs of customers, partners, and suppliers.

At Level 4, the organization has established a clear picture of its entire business value chain, and it can now concentrate on optimizing all aspects of its processes, eliminating waste, and inefficiency. These measures include product and customer profitability, supplier performance, marketing effectiveness, employee productivity, supply chain optimization, customer satisfaction, and others. (See Exhibit 4.6.)

Level 4 indicators include:

- An incremental improvement mind-set is established.
- There is a closed-loop feedback from analysis.
- Information context is based on work flow.
- Experience is shared through collaboration.
- Communities of interest are valued over departments.

Level 5: Innovate

At the "innovate" level, organizations have a culture of innovation and adaptation, which builds on their competencies and uses information to enter new business areas and markets by introducing new products and business

EXHIBIT 4.6   FOURTH LEVEL OF THE INFORMATION EVOLUTION MODEL

Level 4	Human Capital	Knowledge Processes	Culture	Infrastructure
OPTIMIZE	Enterprise group	Extended enterprise	Our partners and us	Extended enterprise systems

models. Companies understand and address the fact that markets eventually begin to commoditize. The organization takes advantage of its collective knowledge, gathers information from a variety of industries, and encourages employee collaboration.

Level 5 focuses on leveraging the understanding of the value creation process that was acquired in Level 4 to replicate that efficiency with new products, in new markets. Organizations at this level understand what they do well, and they apply this expertise to new areas of opportunity to multiply the number of revenue streams flowing into the enterprise. (See Exhibit 4.7.)

Level 5 indicators include:

- New ideas are developed quickly from concept to fruition.
- Access to cross-industry information is available.
- Failures are accepted as learning experiences.
- Ideas are welcomed from anyone in the organization.
- Information is used to forecast and manage new venture risk.

DEFINING THE BI STRATEGY

BICC Perspective on the Information Evolution Model

The five levels of the Information Evolution Model (operate, consolidate, integrate, optimize, and innovate) are all milestones in an organization's evolution in the use of information as a strategic corporate asset for better decision making. It is important for a BICC to understand where its organization currently can be placed with regard to its information maturity and how the BICC needs to evolve to best support the business.

EXHIBIT 4.7   FIFTH LEVEL OF THE INFORMATION EVOLUTION MODEL

Level 5	Human Capital	Knowledge Processes	Culture	Infrastructure
INNOVATE	Dynamic network	Situations matrix	Adaptive groupings	Adaptive systems

In this context, it will be important for the BICC to consider all dimensions of the Information Evolution Model. The Information Evolution Assessment, which uses the Information Evolution Model as its reference model, provides help with this analysis.

Information Evolution Assessment

The BICC should examine these questions:

- What does information maturity mean in the context of your business?
- How mature are you as an organization in use of information as a strategic asset?
- What is your vision?
- How can you translate this vision into a strategy that gives you tangible results?

A systematic process for harmonious growth and smooth transitions starts with an assessment of your organization's current status in the evolutionary process. Without an assessment like that, your BICC runs the risk of focusing on tactical demands as they occur. If that happens, you miss the chance of first obtaining the full picture of BI requirements and then developing the appropriate overall BI strategy.

At SAS, we use the Information Evolution Assessment to help determine the organization's vision and strategy. The assessment takes place in an interactive business setting where consultants work with the client to develop an enterprise strategy so that the client's use of information for decision making can evolve. This assessment uses the Information Evolution Model as the strategic framework and basis of measurement for understanding the maturity of the organization's information-delivery capabilities. The assessment includes interviews with senior business and technical managers and a survey of wider parts of the organization. It explores the client's current BI environment and processes and helps the client establish a vision for using information more effectively by understanding the client's desired BI strategy, goals, and requirements. The results are evaluated and mapped to the Information Evolution Model.

A gap analysis is then performed so that the client sees the distance between its current and its desired maturity level. We assess how the client's human capital, knowledge processes, culture, and infrastructure support the desired strategy. Together, we build an execution strategy for bridging these gaps and moving the organization to the desired level.

The strategy will include an immediate action plan for evolving information-delivery capabilities in the client's organization as well as a prioritized road map for long-term deployment. The goal of the assessment is to provide the client with its BI strategy—the strategy that the client's BICC then will implement and support.

Summary

- Intelligent enterprises are constantly subject to change—at each level, depending on market pressures and internal culture, organizations can be effective users of information. There are cumulative benefits to be gained at every step along the way as an organization matures in its use of information.

- A good starting point is an assessment of the information environment. An assessment looks at the characteristics of the organization and considers where the organization fits, based on business vision, goals, priorities, and culture.

- A key factor is to obtain a view from different levels in the organization (not just from the management perspective) as well as from different business functions on how information currently is used and on what areas need improvement. Keeping the analysis too narrow might result in overlooking interrelationships or missing out on synergies that could be leveraged where requirements from different areas of the business could be or need to be addressed jointly.

- Although there is no "ideal" or appropriate level, organizations must plan how to move from where they perceive they are to where they want to be. Companies should consider all four dimensions—human capital, knowledge processes, culture, and infrastructure—in order to plan how to move forward to accomplish higher degrees of information evolution. These steps should be considered within an overarching, long-term vision.

A comprehensive BI strategy assessment will provide the BICC with a "legitimized" mandate from the business users. This mandate will greatly facilitate buy-in for the BICC when it is up and running.

ENDNOTES

1. Patent pending.
2. For more information, see Jim Davis, Gloria J. Miller, and Allan Russell, *Information Revolution: Using the Information Evolution Model to Grow Your Business* (Hoboken, NJ: John Wiley & Sons, 2006).

Human Capital

OVERVIEW

Now that you have a bird's-eye view of the essentials of Business Intelligence strategy from looking at the Information Evolution Model, let us apply those concepts to the organization in general and to the Business Intelligence Competency Center (BICC) setup in particular. To do that, we will begin with the first dimension of the model and consider what your organization needs to think about to set up a BICC that will be able to mature in each dimension.

Note: The term *human capital* refers to the information skills of individuals within the organization. Specifically, it means the quantifiable aspects of their capabilities, recruitment, training, assessment, and alignment with the organization's goals.

STAFFING THE BUSINESS INTELLIGENCE COMPETENCY CENTER

Choosing the "right" staff for the BICC is, of course, instrumental to its success. It is vitally important to choose individuals who have both a business background and an information technology (IT) background. Why is that so crucial?

BICC should not be just another term for *Support Desk*. The mandate of the BICC must be much wider. The BICC will be entrusted with supplying the organization with vital information for decision making and with enabling the organization to use and interpret the results. A thorough knowledge of the business and the industry, its most pressing issues, its key performance indicators, and the corporate data definitions is crucial for anyone who will fulfill this mandate.

At the same time, of equal importance is an excellent understanding of BI, its possibilities, techniques, and tools, and how they are best used to get to the desired results. The BICC staff can be described as interpreters: translating business issues into IT requirements, translating the results back to the business users who need the information.

Finding both sets of skills in the same individual is rare. This is, however, what makes the BICC an interesting career move. People with business backgrounds learn how to leverage data to more intelligently steer the business; people with technical backgrounds learn how and why the information they deliver has repercussions for business decision making.

What kinds of people are required in the BICC? And, for those people, what are the needed competencies—the skills, knowledge, and behaviors? Note that we use the term *competencies* in the subsequent section to encompass all three of these elements.

Obviously, the mandate of the BICC will determine which roles are required to staff it. So, first you will want to ask: What are the objectives for the BICC, and what are the functional areas it should cover? The answers to those questions will drive your decisions about who is needed to staff the BICC. The next section looks at how the functional areas could be staffed.

Job Roles and Role Descriptions

Exhibit 5.1 lists the core roles that should exist in the BICC in support of the BICC functional areas. There could be additional roles depending on the functional areas that the BICC will cover and depending on what is

EXHIBIT 5.1   CORE ROLES FOR MEMBERS OF THE BICC (IN ORDER OF IMPORTANCE)

Job Role	Primary BICC	Functional Area	Role Description
BICC Manager	BI Program		Promotes the value and the potential of BI in the organization. Is responsible for ensuring that BI projects are aligned with corporate strategy and that they meet business requirements. Acts as a liaison between IT and the business. Establishes and monitors key performance indicators (KPIs) for success of the BI strategy and for the work of the BICC. Manages the BICC, vendor relations, and licensing; sponsors internal user groups; and is responsible for metadata. Manages standards and templates for BI. Negotiates service-level agreements (between BICC and the business units).
Business Analyst	BI Program		Understands the business rules and processes of the current

(continues)

EXHIBIT 5.1 CONTINUED

Job Role	Primary BICC	Functional Area	Role Description
			organization. Informs the project team about how data are currently used in the organization and transformations or business rules that are applied to data. Provides support in understanding the information and further clarity in requirements. Acts as a representative of the business unit managers in day-to-day matters. Has a strong background in statistics, forecasting, and optimization and also has experience in applying these to business problems.
Chief Data Steward	Data Stewardship		Identifies issues and recommends initiatives to address data quality and data integrity. Manages cross-departmental initiatives to address data issues (i.e., defining data ownership, creating data quality improvement programs with incentives, performing business meta-data management). Develops and implements a data management strategy that ensures the delivery of information. Coordinates and guides the data stewardship committee and resolves data integration issues across business units. Monitors and reports on quality of data across the organization. Promotes and advocates sound practices in the capturing, management, dissemination, manipulation, and preservation of data to enable BI. Approves business naming standards in line with defined enterprise standards and develops consistent data definitions, standard calculations, and derivations.

EXHIBIT 5.1   CONTINUED

Job Role	Primary BICC	Functional Area	Role Description
Technical Consultant	Technical Support		Ensures correct technical setup of BI solutions and advises the project team on any connectivity, security, or technical requirements and related topics. Is responsible for the technical implementation of the project, for the project's metadata, and for the technical overview of the project. Understands all technical aspects of the solutions, business systems, and the BI software, and the technical architectures but also has some business skills. Provides second-level technical support for the BICC Service Desk.
Project Manager	BI Program		Ensures that BI projects deliver business value. Manages the day-to-day direction and coordination of the project team and reports on the project status to the project sponsor. Integrates new business changes and ensures alignment of changes to any affected systems if required. Also obtains organizational support and resources for the project (i.e., equipment, software, user accounts, office space, access passes, ID cards).
BI Specialist	BI Program		Understands models and analytical reports and applies them to business uses. Applies the results of the statistical analysis to the business in order to achieve business results. Uses expertise in the given subject area to interpret and apply statistical models.

(continues)

EXHIBIT 5.1   CONTINUED

Job Role	Primary BICC	Functional Area	Role Description
			A summary of the skills of a typical BI specialist:
			• 80% business background and 20% analytical background • Experienced in interpreting and applying statistical models • Functional expertise in the given subject area
			Helps to develop and implement BI solutions and supports users with more advanced tasks that are beyond the skills of a regular BI user. Is very adept in using BI tools.
Warehouse Architect	Data Stewardship		Plans the overall architecture of the solution, including performance considerations, storage repository selections, data schemas, and subject definitions.
			The warehouse architect is responsible for these areas:
			• Subject matter of the data warehouse (DWH) (i.e., the business concepts of the DWH) • Technical aspects of the DWH (i.e., the technical infrastructure of the DWH) • Data aspects of the DWH i.e., the conceptual and logical models of DWH and subsequent data marts)
			Depending on the organization, the role can also be specialized according to the areas as subject matter warehouse architect, technical warehouse architect, or warehouse data architect.
Administrative Assistant	BI Program		Provides administrative support for the BICC. Coordinates and organizes training, liaises with

EXHIBIT 5.1   CONTINUED

Job Role	Primary BICC	Functional Area	Role Description
			software vendors, organizes training needs analyses with vendors, and registers staff for appropriate certifications.
Knowledge Officer BICC	BI Program		Manages the creation of practices, policies, systems and procedures consistent with corporate strategies to maximize the use and retention of explicit and tacit knowledge. Is responsible for the strategies, plans, and implementation of knowledge management practices and programs across all functions and departments of the BICC. Works in tight cooperation with the organization's knowledge office.
Internal Communicator	BI Program		Communicates activities, plans, and progress on current projects, as well as responsibilities and achievements of the BICC to the organization. Coordinates and organizes the organization's information requests to vendors. Supplies, amends, and distributes BI software vendor's information or BI-related information. Creates Web sites, newsletters, presentations, brochures, etc. Organizes third-party visits.
Application Designer/ Developer	BI Delivery		Designs, writes, and tests warehouse programs and applications according to approved design and standards, under the guidance of the warehouse consultant and the warehouse architect. This role could involve one or more individuals specializing in data management or BI delivery.

(continues)

EXHIBIT 5.1   CONTINUED

Job Role	Primary BICC	Functional Area	Role Description
Warehouse Consultant	Data Acquisition		Uses skills in data design and modeling techniques to develop the warehouse according to the proposed design. Applies knowledge of client/server and multi-tiered architecture design to construct and populate the warehouse according to the planned warehouse architecture.
License Administrator	Contract Management		Manages relations between vendors and own organization (contracts [legal], purchasing, system units) regarding licensing issues.
Statistician/ Data Miner	Advanced Analytics		Performs general statistical analysis, forecasting, and optimization. Builds the models and produces the analytical reports. Employs extensive experience as a statistician in such fields as decision trees, cluster analysis, and correspondence analysis to address decision support queries. Selects, explores, and models data to uncover previously unknown patterns.
Training Consultant	Training		Conducts periodic training needs analyses to assess the target audience and to define the most efficient and effective method to provide the training. Designs, develops, and provides training to the organization's employees. Reviews training at each stage to continuously improve its quality and effectiveness.

and what is not covered by other business units or outsourced to an external provider.

It is important to bear in mind that, in reality, one individual would very likely fulfill several of these roles, so the *number of roles* does not necessarily correspond to the *number of people* required to staff the BICC.

The next section presents a list of the names of related roles that could support the BICC from *other parts in the organization*. The definitions for those roles appear in the Appendix, "Other Roles." They are highly related to the BICC work. Some of these roles might be suitable for inclusion in the BICC, but this is a decision to be made on a case-by-case basis.

Finally, the roles that a vendor or consulting company could take on during the setup of a Competency Center appear in Exhibit 5.2.

Note that there may be many factors affecting the decision of which roles would actually be part of the BICC, which ones would be covered elsewhere in the organization, and which ones would be outsourced. The selection presented here therefore needs to be treated as a recommendation only.

EXHIBIT 5.2   ROLES TO DELEGATE TO EXTERNAL SUPPORT (DURING SETUP).

Job Role	Source	Role Description
BICC Consultant	Software vendor, management consulting firm, etc.	Provides advice and assistance during BICC setup.
BICC Liaison	Software vendor	Is the dedicated contact person for the BICC with a particular (software) vendor. Has the following responsibilities: • Is the central point of contact for BICC requests to that vendor. • Coordinates the requests and involves other individuals in the vendor organization as appropriate.
Business Consultant	Software vendor, management consulting firm etc.	Provides advice and assistance in defining the BI strategy and in assuring that the BI solutions align with business goals.
Change Management Consultant	Management consulting firm	Develops and supports the implementation of an organizational change management plan to support implementation of the BICC.

Core BICC Roles. Exhibit 5.1 lists the roles that in our view should exist *inside* the BICC. They are ordered by importance. Based on the fact that we regard BI Program, technical support, and data stewardship as the most crucial functional areas, we think that initially, at an absolute minimum, the BICC should comprise these roles:

- BICC manager
- Business analyst
- Chief data steward
- Technical consultant

Over time, the BICC can be enlarged either by adding more roles to the existing minimum functions or by adding more functional areas to the BICC.

Other Supporting Job Roles. The roles listed in Exhibit 5.1 will likely exist *within* the BICC. Some of the next roles could exist either inside the BICC or be taken over by other business units. Most of them are likely to exist inside your own organization; however, a few could be outsourced to an external provider. Still others, such as the board of directors, will, of course, never be part of the BICC but will need to provide executive support to it.

BUSINESS ROLES
- Advisor to the legal department
- Board of directors
- Business domain expert
- Business executive
- Business users
- Executive sponsor
- Finance officer
- Human resources (HR)

IT ROLES
- Construction manager
- Data manager
- Data quality specialist

- Enterprise information manager
- IT manager and IT operations team
- Project security specialist
- Quality team
- Technical communicator
- Warehouse administrator

More information about these roles can be found in the Appendix. An electronic version of the complete list of roles can be downloaded from the BICC book Web site (see the Preface of this book for details).

External Support. You might decide to ask for outside help when establishing your BICC. Exhibit 5.2 lists external support that might be useful during the setup. When the BICC is up and running, it will very likely still get support from vendors and other external providers, but for the purpose of this book, we restrict the roles here to the ones involved in the setup.

Required Competencies

For each of the roles, it is important to establish which competencies (skills, knowledge, and behaviors) are required. Defining competencies is essential for recruiting and allocating resources, reviewing performance, and training and development of BICC staff. Your organization might already have a competency framework that outlines the competencies required by the different job roles. This framework should be used as a basis to specify the competencies needed for the BICC staff.

The next competency groups should be considered for BICC roles:

- Personal and interpersonal
- Project management
- Leadership and management
- Business and industry
- Business Intelligence (concepts, solution design and development, product-specific competencies)
- Training design and delivery

Each BICC role will need competencies in these areas, but to a varying degree of depth. For each of the roles, you should create a required profile that you then can match with the available resources.

Business-User Training and Coaching

Developing the appropriate competencies for the BICC staff is only part of the successful implementation of a BI strategy. The information consumers (the business users) in the business units also must have a certain level of information skills. In other words, they must have the necessary skills to use information and information technology to perform their jobs effectively (i.e., analytical thinking skills and the ability to use BI software). Business users need to understand which questions they could ask and how the query should be put together to get the desired result. They need to know what data are available to them for analysis and must be able to understand, interpret, and act properly on the results. It is therefore important to analyze training and development needs in the business units, to make sure business users are at the right competency level.

When business users have the necessary skills, they will be able to use BI and BI technology confidently and successfully. The BICC should therefore emphasize business–user education in the area of BI concepts, possibilities, techniques, and tools. Training should happen on a regular basis, but it becomes even more critical as part of the roll-out of new systems and technology to the business. Your investment must pay off—you need to ensure the new software is used efficiently and effectively. Business-user education must be built into the plan for every BI project in the organization and should be subject to regular review.

Summary

- Considerations from a human capital perspective should start with identifying which functions a BICC intends to cover and which roles are needed to support those functions. The next step is to establish which competencies the staff members in those roles need to have to do their jobs.

- Exhibit 5.3 provides a graphical summary of the main points we have laid out.

- In most cases, it cannot be assumed that all individuals already have all the competencies they need, at the appropriate level. A training needs analysis needs to be conducted to determine any current gaps, and a training and development plan needs to be created. Training plans should exist both for the BICC members and for business users. A training plan should state the training objectives and desired outcomes and include these components:
  - Courses (instructor-based, self-paced e-learning, live Web classes)
  - Certifications
  - Coaching and knowledge transfer sessions
  - User groups
  - Publications

EXHIBIT 5.3   WAYS TO STAFF THE BICC

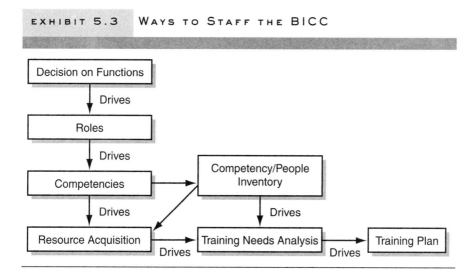

- Information sessions (specifically about how technology can address business issues)

In many of these areas you will work closely with management consultants and BI software vendors. Any external provider will need to have a skill set similar to that of your BICC (i.e., be well versed in business topics and issues that you need to address while having a deep knowledge of the BI technology that deals with these issues).

Knowledge Processes

Overview

One of the key tasks of a Business Intelligence Competency Center is to overcome the information jungle, where information is retrieved and published according to a group's—or most often to an individual's—liking, without any accountable or documented process behind it. This leads to information chaos, where reports from different people do not reconcile or are simply not available, and where all information providers claim that their reports are correct. On a higher level, some agreement might have been reached within a department or business unit, but there is no way of obtaining a corporate view, because different rules, tools, and processes are used, no data cleansing has occurred, and there is no audit trail.

How can a BICC overcome these problems?

The BICC needs to establish knowledge processes to enable a common view across the organization, using consistent rules and standards. That resulting information then needs to be made available to every person in the organization who has a need for it. Corporate rules of data availability and data access rules need to be adhered to.

Note: The term *knowledge processes* refers to processes that deal with these issues:

- How information is generated, validated, and used
- How information is tied to performance metrics and reward systems
- How the organization supports its commitment to the strategic use of information

To be valid for the whole organization, knowledge processes need to be built using a common set of policies, best practices, standards, and governance rules, all of which must adhere to those of the organization.

As details will vary from organization to organization, describing processes in a generic way will by nature be somewhat abstract. Therefore, instead of presenting process templates, this chapter mainly discusses *types* of processes and lists the most important topics that need to be addressed by them. In that way, we clarify the key areas and the corresponding main topics that need to be addressed by the knowledge processes. You can use them as a reference when setting up processes in your organization.

From Individual to Departmental to Enterprise

Ideally, knowledge processes should already be well defined across the organization, with established feedback channels and redefinition processes where necessary. In reality, however, the BICC will be tasked with establishing knowledge processes across individual or departmental barriers.

Even today, information creation sometimes still is solely dependent on individuals in many organizations. Therefore, processes are mostly personal and undocumented, and results depend on individual work styles and preferences. When establishing knowledge processes, care needs to be taken to capture such individual knowledge. Quite often capturing that individual knowledge is the first step before any definition of organizational processes can take place and enterprise standards are agreed on.

Most common today is the scenario where information management and knowledge processes occur on a departmental level. The major issue here is that work is often duplicated, home-grown solutions are in place, and data acquisition is often done outside the business intelligence (BI) system. In this scenario, knowledge processes will be defined, but they are tailored to the individual department's needs, with no input from outside and no common set of standards and definitions. To obtain an organizational view, manual consolidation is necessary. Often such consolidation is complicated by figures from different departments not matching up. In such a situation, the first action to take with regard to knowledge processes is to establish a set of standards and definitions for use with *every* application and department.

When a holistic view of the organization is established, duplicate, overlapping, and inefficient processes become apparent. The next challenge is to encourage and manage change for knowledge processes and establish regular reviews by all concerned parties. Again, the BICC will take a lead here, but the effort will include basically all business units and functions.

KNOWLEDGE PROCESSES IN THE BUSINESS INTELLIGENCE COMPETENCY CENTER'S FUNCTIONAL AREAS

Knowledge processes will not be limited to the BICC but will have a much broader impact on an organization. The BICC, however, normally will have ownership for certain processes that fall into its functional areas.

The key process types are given in the next sections. Many of the items factually describe important aspects that have to be taken into account when those few, but manageable and important, processes are defined and implemented.

Business Intelligence Program

Before information can be made available to the business-user audience, corporate metrics need to be defined with common definitions and agreed business rules. These definitions and business rules need to be standardized across the organization before the information is distributed. These definitions and rules range from simple, tactical metrics such as cash flow, gross margin, total revenue, and net income, to more complex metrics such as financial growth, customer satisfaction, market penetration, internal efficiency, and cost. Eventually the metrics will provide a single corporate view on the organization at any point in time.

When it comes to knowledge sharing, an approach that makes all information available to everybody might seem easiest but is certainly not recommended. Not only would that approach be information overkill, but data access policies will prohibit it. Instead, processes need to be established that ensure that individuals have access to such job-relevant information that they are allowed to see and in a format and through a distribution channel that serves their needs best. On a higher level, feedback and collaboration features will be implemented that allow users to share their insights with others in the same group.

The key areas and the corresponding main topics that need to be addressed by the knowledge processes for the BI Program are listed next. When developing processes, ensure these essentials are covered:

CORPORATE VIEW—DEFINING GLOBAL STANDARDS
- Create an overall organization information picture.
- Determine and standardize information sources.
- Define general metrics.
- Enable collection and consolidation.
- Establish "one version of the truth."

INFORMATION PROCESSES—DISTRIBUTING AND SHARING KNOWLEDGE

- Enable knowledge sharing across the organization.
- Define information audiences and information access rights.
- Define BI infrastructure and standards.
- Establish and implement methodologies and standards.
- Establish and maintain a corporate knowledge base.

INFORMATION PROCESSES—COLLECTING FEEDBACK AND REACTING TO IT

- Create an information program to improve business processes.
- Set targets for improvement initiatives.
- Focus on business improvement initiatives.

BICC INTERNAL PROCESSES

- Do business planning.
- Ensure alignment to the organization's strategic and operational goals.
- Define and monitor BICC related key performance indicators (KPIs).
- Manage organizational change.
- Plan and execute staff development, recruitment, and training.
- Establish billing processes (if the BICC charges users for its services).
- Promote use of the BICC and its services within the organization.

Data Stewardship

Data stewardship focuses on the accuracy of the consolidated information. As this function brings together the technical view on data and the business view on information, it is crucial that all processes are well documented and established in a joint effort between the organization's business and technical units. A first step in this direction is the agreement on and the documentation of a common (i.e., business and technical) set of definitions and standards. The implementation of such standards normally would happen in different steps, most probably starting with manual changes to existing systems. Ultimately, though, processes for data accuracy should not simply exist on paper; they need to be built into the BI infrastructure itself to ensure their consistent use. To be able to do this, the ideal BI infrastructure should be capable of supporting a metalayer linking business and technical metadata that can be used by all components of the infrastructure. Such integration also significantly lowers the maintenance efforts and propagation of changes.

The key areas and the corresponding main topics of data accuracy processes that need to be addressed by the knowledge processes for data stewardship are:

- Agree on data definitions and standards.
- Establish definition verification program.
- Define reconciliation processes.
- Define metadata and business rules.
- Conduct data quality improvements.
- Enable impact analysis and data tracking.
- Ensure communication to and participation of all parties.

Support

One of the roles of a BICC is to provide business-related and technical support to the business-user community. Business-related support might share a first-level support with the technical line, thus providing a single point of contact where the problem will be classified as technical or business related.

Technical support is usually organized in different levels, with the first being the actual call or e-mail recipient with a broad knowledge, followed by a group with deep specialist technical knowledge of the systems, and finally an escalation route to the vendor or other external support providers.

Business-related support differs in such a way that usually there is no vendor or external service provider. If the business support specialist is not able to solve the issue, actions need to be taken in collaboration with the business unit or group the request came from. Another area of business-related support is to provide guidance on how to translate business questions into a problem that can be addressed by technology. Doing this includes assistance in selecting the technology fit to the task and in interpreting the final results. In case of complex analytical tasks, the BICC's advanced analytics function might get involved.

The key areas and the corresponding main topics that need to be addressed by the knowledge processes for support are:

SUPPORT OPERATIONS
- Establish a call-tracking and classification system.
- Establish problem–solving techniques and tools.
- Define an answering and escalation routine.
- Define service-level agreements.

TECHNICAL SUPPORT SPECIFIC
- Establish interfaces to the organization's IT department.
- Collaborate with vendor and external functions.

BUSINESS-SUPPORT SPECIFIC
- Establish interfaces to the organization's business departments.

BI Delivery

The BI delivery function will implement or execute the strategy that has been set by the BI Program function; therefore, a close collaboration is needed and execution processes must follow general rules that are defined in the BI Program's processes. BI delivery owns the BI infrastructure in close collaboration with the other functional areas in the BICC, and in partnership with the organization's information technology (IT) department. Thus, BI delivery is ultimately responsible for all maintenance, change requests, and new projects regarding the BI infrastructure.

The key areas and the corresponding main topics that need to be addressed by the knowledge processes for BI delivery are:

OPERATIONAL PROCESSES
- Carry out infrastructure maintenance.
- Track change requests and new projects.
- Gather user requirements and feedback.
- Execute project management, including technical change management.
- Establish development, testing, and promotion processes.
- Collaborate with IT functions.
- Execute project review and evaluation.

INFORMATION PROCESSES—DELIVERY

- Publish documentation and usage guidelines.

- Determine format, channel, and content appropriate for each user profile.

- Monitor adherence to access restrictions and other rules.

- Monitor and improve performance, clarity, and layout.

- Develop and implement organizational reporting standards.

Data Acquisition

The basic processes that are required concern standardization of data standards, definitional standards, and tool standards. Further, common access permissions and rules need to be established throughout the organization. When this has been achieved, the next level of processes will deal with a range of information management processes, such as metadata management, data modeling, data quality, audit and preventive intervention, and information distribution. At this level, data consistency is achieved and quality information is available to recipients when needed and in a format they prefer, allowing business users to make informed decisions. In addition, accountability is greatly improved as a result of establishing defined processes for the whole organization instead of individual ad hoc processes for each business unit.

The key areas and the corresponding main topics that need to be addressed by the knowledge processes for data acquisition are:

INFORMATION PROCESSES—EXTRACTION OF DATA

- Create interfaces to source systems (normally operational systems).

- Standardize rules and jobs for data extraction.

- Monitor performance and optimization.

INFORMATION PROCESSES—TRANSFORMATION OF DATA

- Create data integration processes.

- Strengthen the role and use of metadata.

- Establish common data definitions across the organization: "One version of the truth."

Advanced Analytics

Within the context of the BICC, advanced analytics processing is offered mainly as an "on-request" service to the business-user community, mainly ad hoc, with additional duties of providing recurring (or standard) analytical reports according to general business needs. Duties also might include internal work, such as scientific research and analytics methodology. Good communication channels with the business units are essential. Advanced analytic research tends to be time-consuming. Resource management is important, especially from a cost perspective.

The key areas and the corresponding main topics that need to be addressed by the knowledge processes for advanced analytics are:

REQUEST MANAGEMENT
- Define analysis scope.
- Evaluate cost versus business benefit.
- Estimate effort for complex tasks.

DATA PREPARATION AND VALIDATION
- Collaborate with data acquisition and data stewardship functions.

RESEARCH AND KNOWLEDGE SHARING
- Establish and implement analytical methodologies, models, and standards.

Training

Whatever needs to be established in terms of training processes depends largely on the extent that training will be conducted by the BICC itself or outsourced to an external provider. It is particularly important that a thorough training needs analysis for the BICC staff as well as for the business users be conducted to ensure that the training corresponds to the requirements of the training recipients.

Another important but generally less formal way of disseminating knowledge is knowledge transfer. Knowledge transfer differs from formal training in that it provides multiple individuals with a forum to share tacit knowledge or experiences they have gained on a particular topic in an interactive method, whereas training provides instruction on a selected topic in a structured format.

The key areas and the corresponding main topics that need to be addressed by the knowledge processes for training are:

ASSESSMENT AND REVIEW
- Review training needs in the BICC and for business users.
- Examine training needs in relation to specific projects.
- Determine training types and media (instructor-based training, e-learning, coaching, appropriate literature).
- Develop training plan.
- Evaluate training.

ORGANIZING TRAINING
- Identify instructor or instructors.
- Create training material.
- Organize course logistics.
- Interface with vendors and other external training suppliers.

KNOWLEDGE TRANSFER
- Organize formal or informal forums, peer-to-peer sessions, etc.
- Chair, moderate, or facilitate sessions.
- Establish communities of practice and practice leaders.
- Disseminate knowledge to individuals.

Vendor Contracts Management

Knowledge processes for vendor contracts management will involve an organization's legal and procurement units. Close collaboration is essential, and knowledge processes are likely to be jointly owned by the BICC and one or both units.

The key areas and the corresponding main topics that need to be addressed by the knowledge processes for vendor contracts management include:

VENDOR RELATIONSHIP MANAGEMENT AND STRATEGIC DEVELOPMENT
- Validate vendor portfolio with strategic and operational goals.
- Collaborate with strategic vendors.

LICENSE MANAGEMENT
- Monitor adherence to vendor license regulations.
- Review and optimize license usage.
- Renegotiate contracts.

REQUESTS FOR PROPOSAL, BIDS PROCESSES
- Review and create input for proposals, contracts, and so forth.
- Conduct vendor evaluation and approval.

Summary

- Knowledge processes play an important role in achieving a single version of the truth and delivering the right information to the right people, at the right time.
- Processes need to be incorporated into the overall BI infrastructure wherever possible to ensure that they are followed throughout: This is especially important for any treatment of the original data, such as applying business rules or consolidations or for matching up technical and business metadata.
- Often multiple functions within the BICC and from across the organization need to work together on processes that cut across functional units. It is important that the organization supports and facilitates this collaboration.
- The idea of a BICC is often introduced when the need arises to bring information management and knowledge processes to the next level, from the individual to the departmental level or, more often, from a departmental to a true organizational view.
- The organizational view is supported by knowledge processes spanning different departments, using consistent definitions and standards, adopting quality processes across the organization, and creating metrics and key performance indicators that can be tracked consistently. It is a key task of the BICC to establish such knowledge processes and ensure that key topics are addressed.

Culture

OVERVIEW

Setting up a Business Intelligence Competency Center in your organization *will* bring about change:

- People will change jobs or responsibilities.
- The way in which individual departments work together will be organized differently.
- New processes will be introduced.

As a result, some people might gain power, while others might lose power. Preparing for these changes requires careful planning and an analysis of all the implications that the BICC setup will have on the organization. In this context, is it better to set up the BICC as a central team in a separate business unit or as a virtual team that includes representatives from different departments?

Introducing a common Business Intelligence (BI) architecture will require that the staff learn new tools and technologies and do away with "the old way" of doing things. Business users will have access to true business intelligence—perhaps for the first time—and this will increase their appetite for more. In the midterm or longer, this common architecture will raise a discussion around the BICC's funding. Thus, different opportunities for funding models should be examined.

Another important aspect to look at is how to evaluate the success of the BICC. But what should the performance metrics be? Some of them will be tangible, some intangible.

Further, methodology and standards need to be created, and compliance needs to be ensured. Best practices, techniques, programs, documentation, and the like should be collected and shared. Knowledge management plays an important role in this context.

Note: The term *culture* refers to the organizational and human influences on information flow—the moral, social, and behavioral norms of corporate culture (as shown in the attitudes, beliefs, and priorities of its members), regarding the use and value of information as a long-term strategic corporate asset.

ORGANIZATIONAL SETUP AND FUNDING

Central Versus Virtual BICC

To be able to fulfill its mandate for acting as a bridge between information technology (IT) and the organization, it is clear that the BICC team has to be cross-functional. It must have representatives from both IT and the business. It must have executive sponsorship to be successful in its strategic role.

Many organizations wrestle with the question "Do we want a BICC that is permanent with a physical team, or is it better to have a virtual team that includes employees in several business units and IT organizations?" The virtual BICC is least "disturbing" to the current organizational structure. The idea here is that, while reporting structures remain unchanged, staff members from different departments are nominated as virtual members of the BICC and act as representatives from their business units. They might be filling this role part-time or full-time. This approach also guarantees that the BICC members can stay close to the day-to-day business. (See Exhibit 7.1.)

Considering these advantages, organizations might prefer a "virtual" to a fully staffed BICC. A move to a functional unit would mean an internal reorganization and shifting of budgets. The main disadvantage of a virtual

EXHIBIT 7.1   VIRTUAL BICC

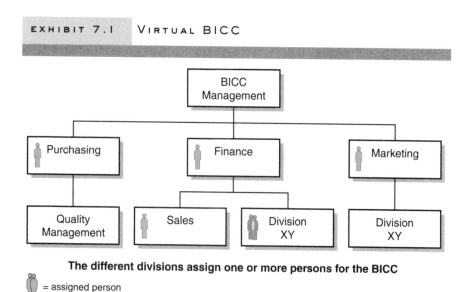

The different divisions assign one or more persons for the BICC

= assigned person

BICC is, however, that there is a risk of limited accountability, communication, and alignment between the members of the BICC, which increases difficulties to share experiences with the different functional teams. Also, as always in virtual teams, each member is first and foremost committed to the priorities, goals, and objectives of his or her direct management. Therefore, the objectives of the BICC and the functional department to which an individual belongs could be in conflict. In a virtual model, management buy-in and support from the individual business units needs to be very high, and both groups need to respect and comply with the work of the BICC, even more than it would be the case in a central model.

A "central" BICC is one that is set up as its own functional unit. Individuals who join the BICC report to the BICC manager. In this model, roles and responsibilities, reporting lines, and the place the BICC has in the organization are very clearly defined. These factors can make it easier for the BICC to be assertive in situations where there is a conflict of interest between the various business units, for example, with regard to BI project priorities. This is especially true if the BICC reports to the executive level and therefore has a very high visibility in the organization. Furthermore, it is likely that staff members belonging to a central BICC will be more independent and less prone to act in the interest of any particular business unit. (See Exhibit 7.2.)

EXHIBIT 7.2   CENTRAL BICC

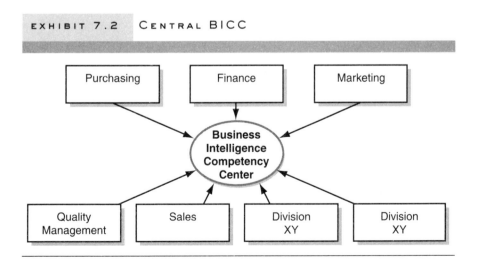

If the decision is in favor of a central BICC, there should be a sound organizational change management process to support the transition. Organizational change management and its importance in the context of forming BICCs are covered later in this chapter.

Sometimes it will be difficult to form a BICC as a centralized, separate organizational unit. Political and budgetary constraints can get in the way.

Regardless of the structure of the organization, the BICC should have executive sponsorship and should report to the executive level, for example, to the chief intelligence officer (CIO) or to the chief operational officer (COO). The goal must be the alignment of BI goals across various functional areas, in support of the organization's strategy.

To find the solution that is right for your organization, you might consider combining the two approaches and adopting a model in which the people working in the BICC would be exchanged on a regular basis. This approach would help ensure that the individual BICC staff members are not alienated from business topics.

Every BICC model has its own challenges and advantages. The first step should be to define the BI strategy and the processes needed to accomplish that strategy. Working out the BI strategy and processes will help define which BICC "model" would be most advisable and feasible in the current organizational culture.

BICC Funding Models

Who is going to pay for the BICC's work? Having the right funding model is important for the BICC's success and will affect the business case. A number of different models come to mind; the selection of any one of them will be influenced greatly by the organizational culture and by how other departments might already be cross-charging for their services. Here are several ideas:

- Costs can be treated as overheads, and then all departments can use the BI services. The disadvantage of this approach is that it is more difficult to show the economic value of the BICC, at the risk of having an underappreciated BICC or reducing it to a second-level technical support group for BI.

- If an internal billing system (including time tracking) is used, the users are charged for help given on each project and analysis. This model shares costs fairly because heavy users pay more than light users. However, this approach can limit the growth and use of the BICC by the different user groups because people might try to use the charges as an excuse not to get involved.

- A subscription-based billing model reduces barriers for users. It assigns costs across each user group, depending on the anticipated usage of the BICC. However, subscription fees would need to be compared to actual use and adjusted on a regular basis.

In the longer term, the subscription-based model that assigns costs to all Competency Center users, based on usage levels, seems to be fairest. It promotes the optional usage and work with the Competency Center. It shows the center's economic value; and at the same time, the costs are distributed fairly and will not deter business users.

However, as mentioned earlier, the funding model that will be chosen will depend to a large extent on whatever fits with the organizational culture. Whatever funding model is chosen, the most important consideration is that it should not in any way be a barrier to BICC usage.

PERFORMANCE METRICS

In deciding on the goals, objectives, setup, and operations of the BICC, consider the performance metrics or measures for the BICC. Metrics should be relevant to the business value-add and the efficiency the organization can expect from the BICC. Identifying the relevant metrics early on will allow some focus in getting buy-in and commitment for the BICC, in deciding on its operational model, and in communicating about its performance. The BICC will be able to better influence and measure its organizational impact after it becomes mature and established. Therefore, be careful not to establish metrics that are too difficult to measure.

Intangible Benefits

The organization will receive a number of benefits by setting up a BICC. Although these metrics might not be financially quantifiable, they will be relevant for highlighting and sharing the performance of the BICC. (See Exhibit 7.3.)

EXHIBIT 7.3 BICC BENEFITS (INTANGIBLE)

Accuracy	Increases the quality of information available for decision making
	Decreases error rates or improves quality of information
Compatibility	Eliminates additional investments by being compatible with existing operations, facilities, equipment, data
	Eliminates retraining or defers staff costs by being compatible with existing skills and competencies available in the organization
	Achieves a shorter implementation time frame by supporting existing work processes and procedures
Efficiency	Consumes a minimal amount of resources
	Increases processing capabilities
IT performance	Increases resource throughput, decreases response times, increases number of transactions
Maintainability	Increases the maintainability of the solution by a functional unit
	Reduces the need for supervision
Morale	Increases the morale of employees so that they can focus on more fulfilling work
Portability	Eliminates specific rework by being easily portable to different computing environments
Quality	Allows for producing a higher-quality product
Reliability	Reduces unnecessary costs by meeting stated conditions and availability requirements
Residual value	Maintains its financial value longer than needed by the project
Security	Decreases the chance of fraud, misuse of resources, theft
Service life	Extends the service life and eliminates the need for replacement
Staff productivity	Increases rate of production, decreases number of staff previously needed, produces more with the same staff
Upgradeability	Eliminates reinvestment by being usable with newer or larger hardware
Versatility	Provides additional capacity and capabilities beyond those required for the immediate project

Tangible Business Benefit

The overarching goal for the BICC is to leverage the use of information and BI in the organization. The metrics or measures in this area will vary greatly, based on the types of functions that use BI as well as how and for what purposes BI is used within the organization. Thus, each program, project, or service is likely to have a different set of business metrics.

Therefore, you will want to consider now how to determine the metric and how to determine the BICC's contribution to the performance against the metric. For a specific business project, program, or service, the business user making the request will know precisely the business metric that will be affected. You might have to coax the information out of the business user by asking a series of questions.

Each metric needs to have an evaluation of the expected revenue impact or cost contribution. This evaluation usually will be determined based on a few key business drivers, for example, cost per user.

Finally, when the project or service is operational, a method needs to be established to determine how and when to follow up on the benefits realized by it. Establishing this process allows the BICC to follow up and traces its contribution to the organization's performance.

Tangible Operational Efficiency

For operational efficiency, the primary metrics and measures are centered around leveraging the BI infrastructure across the organization so that it will have a broader benefit to the business. The BICC can influence four of the quantifiable benefits for operational efficiency:

1. *Increased number of BI users.* A change in the number of BI users can be a good indicator of whether and how the BI strategy is taken up within the organization. Such a measure can be evaluated based on the number of people using the BI infrastructure or through a periodic survey of the business-user community. An increase in the number of BI users usually indicates that the BI strategy is being leveraged more throughout the organization.

2. *Increased decision-making speed.* Just as the BI strategy should support the organization in making fact-based business decisions, the BICC should help business users with getting responses to business-relevant

questions in the shortest amount of time possible. The types of services and support offered by the BICC will determine its role in providing such answers. Nevertheless, the BI strategy should support reducing the time between question and response. A change in the turn-around time can be measured by evaluating the time it used to take from an initial business question being posed to having the answer provided. This metric should not be about changes in IT response times but about the time it takes business users to retrieve answers to business questions.

3. *Increased staff efficiency.* Changes in the cost of the staff required for operating, managing, and maintaining the BI infrastructure would be a consideration for measuring the efficiency of the BICC's performance. However, a more relevant or important metric is the increase in staff efficiency due to reuse of ideas, concepts, and techniques from different parts of the business (or externally) that is facilitated by the BICC. This reuse metric can be difficult to measure as the BICC will be a facilitator by bringing people together to share knowledge and experience or being the broker of such information into the organization. Such a metric could be evaluated through a survey to the user community to determine how much of the provided information, techniques, concepts, and ideas shared through services offered by the BICC has been reused. For the items brokered by the BICC, a simple calculation using hourly staff costs saved per item shared could be created.

4. *Reduced software costs.* Normally, the discussion about software costs considers the acquisition costs of the software and support. However, there are additional costs for designing, developing, testing, maintaining, and running BI applications. Including such items means a discussion on the total cost of ownership (TCO) for the BI software that is extremely relevant to the BICC. The BICC will have a large degree of responsibility for providing services and support for the BI software and for getting the appropriate funding.

Another aspect to software costs relates to the depth and breath of the software's capabilities. If the BI software has abilities needed for the short term and long term as well as capabilities across a number of different functional units, a need to retool and repurchase with each new service or support request made to the BICC is eliminated.

Such scalability will reduce the overall procurement costs for the organization and should be considered as part of the software cost savings.

Any discussions about cost savings must be balanced by including a discussion about realizing business value and reaching quick payback periods. Both costs and generated business value are components in calculating return on investment (ROI), and both are needed to constitute a convincing business case. If the BICC neglects the business value discussion, the business and corporate management may overlook the business benefits that the BICC could provide.

Business Benefits

Here is a list of examples of business benefits (arranged by industry) that might be achieved through the implementation of BI solutions, projects, and services. The list is not exhaustive—its purpose is to provide business users with some detail on potential business improvements they could gain through BI, with the help of the BICC.

BANKING
- Detect misuse of credit card accounts.
- Determine increase or decrease of client credit line.
- Facilitate compliance with anti–money-laundering regulations.
- Improve mortgage credit risk assessment.
- Increase automatic loan processing.
- Increase conversion rates.
- Increase credit check and customer ratings for each branch.
- Reduce appraisal costs.
- Reduce churn rate.
- Reduce empty period for cash machines.
- Reduce mortgage default rate.
- Reduce bank robberies.
- Save time and resources in reaching regulator compliance.

ENERGY AND UTILITIES
- Eliminate nonrelevant notifications.
- Enable more options in the planning process.
- Enhance decision making and cost control.

- Improve key areas of the business and its operations.
- Reduce material and personnel costs.
- Reduce remote workforce presence on platforms.
- Reduce the number of work orders generated.
- Reuse existing infrastructure.
- Streamline the administrative load and cycle.

GOVERNMENT AND EDUCATION

- Increase due tax collection.
- Increase financial aid packages to most qualified students.
- Increase fraud conviction rate.
- Minimize the costs of assistance.
- Optimize resources allocation.
- Reduce cost per case.
- Reduce scientific analysis time.

INSURANCE

- Decrease policy lapses.
- Improve underwriting.
- Increase campaign response rate.
- Increase cross-selling.
- Increase growth rates in closing cross-selling opportunities.
- Increase retention of profitable customers.
- Minimize healthcare operational costs.
- Predict lapses in coverage.
- Reduce fraudulent claims.
- Reduce policy cancellations.

MANUFACTURING

- Improve business performance.
- Optimize inventory levels.
- Predict and prevent manufacturing process problems.
- Prevent supplier discrepancies.

- Reduce back orders.
- Reduce lead times.
- Reduce reporting times.
- Reduce scrap losses.
- Reduce spending.
- Save staff time.
- Increase control on cost.

RETAIL

- Improve accuracy in predicting costs.
- Improve campaign rates.
- Increase customer activity.
- Increase customer loyalty.
- Increase customer response rate.
- Increase return per campaign.
- Increase revenue per customer.
- Increase revenue to direct marketing expense ratio.
- Increase sales.
- Increase control over campaign activities and costs.
- Reduce direct mail costs.
- Reduce time to analyze customer behavior.

TELECOMMUNICATIONS

- Automate and streamline campaign management process.
- Improve accuracy of suspension.
- Improve customer behavior understanding.
- Improve personalization of product and service offerings.
- Increase average revenue per user (ARPU).
- Increase response rates on targeted campaigns.
- Increase telesales success rate.
- Increase the number of customer interactions.
- Maintain reliable networks and services.

- Prevent fraud.
- Reduce churn rate.
- Reduce the number of low-lifetime-value customers.
- Win back leavers.

KNOWLEDGE MANAGEMENT

Business Intelligence Competency Centers, by definition, provide knowledge to other business units. The BICC staff depends on various knowledge sources, such as:

- Knowledge they have gained during their career (possibly from outside the organization)
- Knowledge obtained during prior work with the business units
- Knowledge researched and built specifically for a given project

As part of their work, BICCs transfer knowledge or expertise using Knowledge Management (KM) principles to those parts of the organization that need it to use BI effectively.

The following overview will show you some of those principles and give you examples of successful KM initiatives that SAS runs. You might want to consider these initiatives for your own organization.

If your organization already has a KM program, we highly recommend that the BICC team work closely with it and exchange ideas with those who run it.

What Is Knowledge Management?

Knowledge Management is concerned with using to best advantage the knowledge and experiences that have been gained across an organization. This can be done by collecting, storing, and distributing information as well as by connecting people to enable sharing of tacit experiences. A KM program enables the organization to benefit from individual as well as collective knowledge assets gained in the past. Since these assets include highly intangible ones, any KM strategy addresses three major aspects:

Human capital or culture

Knowledge processes

Infrastructure

The human capital or culture aspect encompasses everything dealing with the person, with the organization's culture, and with how a group of people can reach a common goal. Communities of practice play a very important part here. They will be discussed in more detail later in this chapter.

Knowledge processes ensure that providing knowledge and finding knowledge is consistent, timely, effective, and repeatable.

Infrastructure plays an important enabler role but should not be the main focus if a KM strategy is to be successful. Likewise, at times technology can also stand in the way of effective knowledge sharing.

Topics that are often addressed in the KM arena include:

- *Human resources (HR):* Skills management (resource planning, Yellow Pages systems, expert locator), resource exchange (temporary engagements or assignments), resource development (personal development and career paths using competency frameworks)
- *Product development and customization:* Technical tools exchange within and across job functions, feedback loops for product development (direct feedback, bug tracking, workarounds, knowledge system contribution ratings)
- *Customer:* 360-degree view of the customer (sales and services touchpoints, win/loss findings, project experiences, references, training needs, customer support requests, product license records)
- *Marketing:* competitor knowledge, references
- *Back-office functions:*
  - Supporting practices over organizational borders (departmental, geographic)
  - Documenting processes, data, and applications
  - Working efficiently with alliance partners, suppliers, and other external providers

It is possible to have a separate system for each of these topics. However, it makes sense to cross-link related systems intelligently. Consider adding a team that provides not only technical support but also process support. This support team should administer the system from the business viewpoint, connect people who are looking for something specific, build business processes to use the systems (consume and contribute), train users, advertise news and new entries, report on successes, and so forth.

What Does Knowledge Management Mean for the Organization?

Knowledge Management enables the organization to get easy access to:

- Ideas and experiences
- People
- Repeatable results

People are best able to deal with a situation when they have some experience or idea to compare it to. The aim of KM is to gain access to the widest base of such ideas and experiences. Knowledge Management initiatives can give you direct access to a solution for your problem or point you to a person who has relevant experience in the area and who might be able to help you.

Communities of Practice

A community of practice (CoP) is a voluntary group of people who are drawn together by a shared interest, passion, or area of expertise. Communities of practice can meet regularly face-to-face or virtually via e-mail or phone. They can use other technologies to support their work, such as virtual office and meeting room. They freely share knowledge and expertise, thus promoting information dissemination, group learning, best practice development, and so forth. Communities of practice are unlike teams or work groups, which tend to be task-specific and have formal requirements for membership. They have an informal membership that is often fluid and self-organizing in nature. The CoP concept is certainly one that could be interesting for BICCs.[1]

SAS' Internal Knowledge Management Initiatives

Knowledge Management has been a topic within SAS for over a decade. Even before the term was becoming fashionable, at the beginning of the 1990s, SAS had an intranet, discussion groups and lists, communities of experts, and technical exchange. SAS had already implemented many of the principles for dealing with knowledge workers that have gotten a lot of attention recently.

In 1997 a formal group, the SAS International Knowledge Office, was founded. It has been instrumental in initiating and guiding the development of a number of worldwide Knowledge Management initiatives, including these:

- *Employee Skills Database (ESDB):* The ESDB captures the skills of SAS employees worldwide so that the appropriate expert for any topic can quickly be identified and contacted. The ESDB therefore is used extensively by SAS internal Resource Sharing program, which helps to resource projects worldwide. In addition, the database represents a skills inventory and allows SAS to plan resource demand.[2]

- *Common Document Index (CDI):* The CDI is a collection of project-related documents from and for all SAS offices. Each entry serves as a pointer to experiences gained and to people within SAS.

- *ToolPool:* ToolPool is a collection of tools (e.g., whole applications, utilities, and code snippets) and technical tips for application development. These tools are shared by SAS employees globally to shorten development times in projects.[3]

- *Yellow Pages:* The Yellow Pages system provides a "who's who" of SAS employees across the globe. It also contains information about the communities of practice that exists internally at SAS. Currently there are more than 70 registered CoPs on different topics.

- *Work Groups:* Work groups bring together a number of individuals in a selected community from around the region to share knowledge, experiences, case studies, and lessons learned around selected topics. SAS International runs more than 1,000 of these sessions per year.

Some of those initiatives have been documented in case studies that you might find useful in gathering ideas for your own organization.[4]

Additionally, SAS has been very active in international forums like IBM's Institute for Knowledge Management (1999–2003). SAS was invited to become a permanent member of the Harvard Learning and Innovations Laboratory (LILA) round table in 2003. In 2005 SAS started to participate in the Babson College Working Knowledge Research Center.

Combining external research and experiences around KM with the internal expertise on the topic was the basis for producing an advanced and very successful KM program.

CHANGE MANAGEMENT

This section deals with managing change effectively. Setting up a BICC to align infrastructure, human capital, knowledge processes, and culture can represent a significant organizational change that potentially affects these areas:

- Vision, strategy, and direction
- Systems and structures
- Organizational culture
- Employee work, behavior, and competencies

In this context, you will want to introduce Change Management processes to ensure organizational objectives and strategies regarding the implementation of a BICC are met and that the commitment of employees is gained and maintained before, during, and after its implementation. Consultants working closely with you on the positioning and deployment of the BICC should bring a good understanding of Change Management issues and how change will affect your organization.

We will look at Change Management from two perspectives:

Your organization's perspective

SAS' perspective

Change Management in the Context of a BICC

Most organizations experience change on a continual basis. Change can be caused by any of the following:

- New strategy, direction, leadership
- New organizational structures
- Reshaping the culture or operating environment
- Incorporating new technology, systems, production, or business processes
- Pressure from competition
- Mergers, acquisitions, joint ventures, breakups
- Downsizing
- Expansion in markets, technologies, offerings

What Is Change Management? Change Management is the practice of ensuring that all changes affecting an organization are carried out in a planned and organized manner. Change Management includes these actions:

- Ensuring that there is a business reason for each change
- Developing business justification and obtaining approval
- Assessing the impact, cost, benefit, and risk of proposed changes on the business and human resources
- Managing and coordinating change implementation
- Monitoring and reporting on implementation
- Having contingency plans for any "ripple effect" the change might cause
- Reviewing and closing

Change Management can be either reactive, in which case management is responding to the impact of external factors, or proactive, in which case management is initiating the change from within in order to achieve a desired goal.

To be effective, Change Management should be multidisciplinary, touching all aspects of the organization, because implementing new structures, systems, and processes always affects people and their motivation. Change almost always involves dealing with some form of resistance to change. Change is a critical human resource issue, affecting motivation and activities. Therefore, attitudes toward change result from a complex interplay of emotional and cognitive processes.

On the positive side, change is seen as an opportunity for progress, innovation, and growth. On the negative side, change can be seen as a source of instability, unpredictability, anxiety, and stress.

Change Management can ensure that standardized methods, processes, and procedures are used for all changes to facilitate the efficient transition from the current state to the future desired state. Close liaison between implementation project managers and change sponsors or managers is required. Resistance to change can be diminished by Change Management processes that promote excitement and confidence in those affected by the change.

Why Change Management Is Important. When introducing a BICC, it is important to consider carefully the way change is managed. If you do not have effective Change Management processes in place, projects will encounter difficulties with successful implementation. Typical operational factors that may be affected by the implementation of a BICC include:

- Management practices
- Organizational structure and systems
- Policies and procedures
- Budget or financial constraints
- Recruitment, selection, or related human resource issues
- Job or task requirements
- Individual competencies and performance
- Working atmosphere and employee motivation
- Individual or group power, influence, and attitudes
- Individual or group performance

Although generally each change situation will be different for each organization, a number of common operational factors help ensure that the BICC change process stands the greatest chance of success. In one example, an organization introduced the equivalent of a BICC as part of an enterprise-wide BI solution. This strategy resulted in making planned changes to management practices, infrastructure, systems, procedures, jobs, performance, and competency development. The changes were effectively planned and managed, resulting in the successful optimization of BI in the organization.

Organizational Barriers to Change. Change initiatives such as the implementation of a BICC are often undertaken as part of a wider change initiative. Typical barriers to introducing change can include:

- Introducing a change that focuses too narrowly on one aspect of the organization. For example, a change may consider implementing a BICC structure within the organization, but may fail to introduce the systems and employee development required to support such a structure.
- Lack of strong project and people management disciplines can lead to slippage in project delivery, which can adversely affect the achievement of desired outcomes for the BICC project.
- Insufficient training—for example, in new skills, project management, and Change Management—also influence negatively the effectiveness of any change initiative.

- Lack of vision, mission, and an effective communication strategy can lead to little or no understanding of the change and its benefits, increasing a sense that the change is being imposed, and resulting in greater resistance than anticipated.
- Lack of transparent leadership and buy-in can also greatly affect commitment and motivation regarding the planned change.

Individual and Group Resistance to Change. Resistance to change can be defined as an individual or group engaging in acts to ignore, block, or disrupt an attempt to introduce change. Resistance itself can take many different forms, including subtle undermining of change initiatives, critical remarks, withholding of information, or not using the systems and processes put in place.

Resistance to change can therefore be considered along two dimensions:

Resistance to the content of change, for example, to the specific changes in technology caused by the introduction of a BICC.

Resistance to the processes of change caused by the BICC. This concerns the way a change is introduced rather than the object of the change itself. An example would be restructuring job roles without prior consultation with the employees affected by the restructuring.

Potential reasons for resistance include loss of control, shock of the new and affection for the old, uncertainty, inconvenience, threat to status, fear of a lack of competency. It is important to try to diagnose the cause of resistance, as this will help focus the effort in trying to reduce or remove the problem.

Understanding Organizational Change. In general terms, a change program should satisfy these criteria:

- It should describe the change process to all people involved and explain the reasons why the changes are occurring. The information should be complete, unbiased, reliable, transparent, and timely.
- It should be designed to implement the change effectively while being aligned with organizational objectives, external trends, and employee perceptions and feelings.
- The program should provide support to employees as they deal with the change, and wherever possible involve the employees directly in the change process itself.

A useful starting point to understand how change affects organizations is the congruence model of organizational behavior by Nadler, Tushman, and Nadler, shown in Exhibit 7.4.[5]

The model is a strategic planning and organizational development tool based on identifying an organization's performance in relation to its strategy. The model shows the need to align four key organizational components:

People: Competencies, motivation, behavior (human capital)

Work activities: Tasks, methods, information (knowledge processes)

Culture: Norms, values, informal networks, roles, power, "the way we do things around here"

Structure and systems: Organizations, strategic grouping, operating systems, and teams (infrastructure)

Change Management will require implementation of the desired change while continuing to meet the ongoing demands of the business. The model can be applied to a BICC that seeks to bring BI "congruence" to the strategies, structures, systems, and processes behind the organization's information delivery. The organization will in turn change its culture regarding Information Management and its impact on decision making.

EXHIBIT 7.4   ORGANIZATION BEHAVIOR MODEL

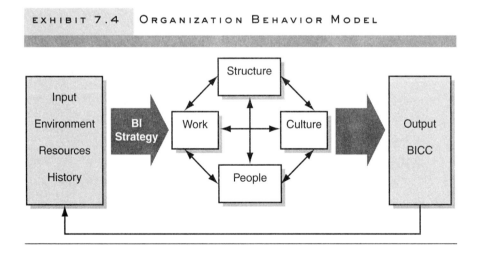

Managing Change in the BICC Context

When implementing a BICC, a step-by-step approach can be applied using the typical Current State → Transition State → Future State Framework as shown in Exhibit 7.5, which is based on Kurt Lewin's Model for Organizational Change.

Current State: Setting Up the Change Management Process. The executive sponsor of the initiative sets out the business reason and drivers behind introducing a BICC, based on the strategic framework, objectives, and operational benefits of having a BICC within the organization. The SAS Information Evolution Assessment offers a business-focused collaboration and analysis that drives this assessment and defines the direction and reasons for the change. It is also an excellent way to involve and give staff a sense of contributing to the change process.

These eight steps can then be taken to set up the change process:

1. Identify and bring together key stakeholders who will be involved and directly affected by the project.

2. Establish time frames, resources, necessary budget, and anticipated ROI, including the performance indicators that will show that the BICC has been integrated successfully into the business.

EXHIBIT 7.5   ORGANIZATIONAL CHANGE (ADAPTED FROM KURT LEWIN)

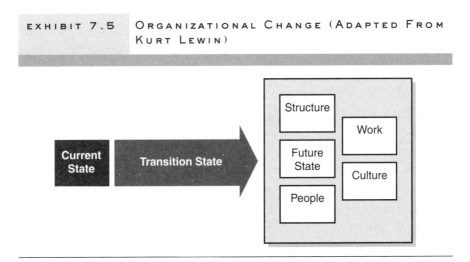

Source: Adapted from Thomas G. Cummings and Edgar F. Huse, *Organization Development and Change*, 4th ed. (St. Paul, MN: West Publishing Company, 1989).

3. Work together with Business, Human Resources, and technical stakeholders to clarify the benefits of the change, and its impact on their respective domains within the organization.

4. Establish and prioritize implementation steps, providing a more detailed review of costs, resources, and time frames.

5. Obtain the green light to go ahead with the project, based on the outcomes of the four previous steps.

6. Develop a communication strategy, aimed at motivating those affected by the change to accept and support its implementation during the transition state.

7. Assign project leaders to communicate and initiate the proposed change in their domains, and to manage the project outcomes.

8. Identify required positions and competency profiles.

Managing the Transition State

As the congruence model makes clear, major changes in one part of the organization will create changes elsewhere. Often most difficulties arise when implementation steps are taken during the transition period from current to future state—namely, when you are attempting to put strategy into action.

Typically, the characteristics of the transition state will depend on the nature of the change and the culture of the organization. However, the transition state begins when the first rumor of change enters the organizational "grapevine." The transition state is the time in which the most resistance will be encountered and the most problems generated. Typical factors are:

- Anxiety and a sense of uncertainty
- Power and politics

Anxiety and a Sense of Uncertainty. A sense of uncertainty and instability usually is generated during the transition state, which can adversely affect performance—especially if your employees are expected to let go of the known and move to an uncertain future. Uncertainty is generally fed by a lack of concrete information about the change taking place, how it will be managed, and how it will shape the future value of their skills and contributions. The higher the levels of anxiety become, the less people are able to listen, consider, and understand the purpose and value of the change. Employees feel locked in a reactive change process and feel that they have no control over the situation.

However, a well-managed change process can reduce uncertainty and produce a positive reaction from those affected during the transition state. If the change communication strategy directly addresses the question "What does this mean for me?" your employees are more likely to understand the new opportunities that are available for the organization as well as for themselves.

Power and Politics. Every organization will have formal and informal groups and a set of individuals where power and influence is distributed, and where people have different interests and perspectives. Major change programs can disturb or threaten the distribution of power, creating increased political activities, even competition for scarce resources and influence. Those who have significant power worry about losing it, might act defensively, and may seek to maintain the status quo. Those who have less power see new openings and might begin maneuvering for a better position as a result of the change.

Political activity is most intense when the impending changes strike at the existing core values and culture of the organization.

Proactively Managing the Change Process During Transition

Management of the change process can be based on the factors within the congruence model, broken down into two halves:

Structure and work

Culture and people

Structure and Work. Building the BICC structures and systems and integrating them into the BI processes of the organization require management functions that manage the resources engaged in the work and the systems they affect. These functions involve:

- Tracking and report the changes taking place in the transition stage of introducing the BICC.

- Ensuring that all agreed changes to business processes and systems are implemented.
- Ensuring that the quality of BI, data management, and data integrity is monitored and reported, so that stability and consistency is maintained during the transition period.

Culture and People.[6] Changes to the processes underpinning the BICC strategy must be tackled in a proactive way, even if the steps appear both complex and time consuming. Some of the steps to consider are:

Employing leadership behavior to create support. The visible actions of respected leaders are crucial to creating widespread support for the change in your organization. These actions include the ways in which key leaders use rewards and punishment, how they employ language and symbols, and how they represent the value of the change taking place. During the transition, more than at any other time, every leader has to "walk the talk."

Proactively dealing with resistance and conflict. Key players should be targeted at the outset and a range of techniques employed either to engage those who can be helpful or to lessen the impact of those who could damage the initiative. Effort should be made to empathize with those who are experiencing the change directly. The most critical technique is building participation and involvement in implementing the change. The more staff members are engaged in a process, the more successful the transition will be. Participation brings these benefits:

- A sense of ownership rather than perceiving change as something that someone else is doing to them
- A sense of understanding through working within the project—both in terms of understanding the business strategy and value of the BICC and in terms of learning new competencies
- A process of knowledge sharing, a diversity of information ideas and different perspectives that can potentially improve on the original plan

Getting key players involved and winning their support can begin with a small group that is entrusted with and shows total commitment to the project, using the ripple effect to gradually engage other groups, increasing levels of participation within the organization.

At the next level, persuasive strategies sometimes can be used to win the support of staff members who need to be convinced of the value of the change during the transition state. They might be won over through a sense of company loyalty or sense of duty, or belief in the value of the project. Other incentives include new career opportunities, new roles and responsibilities, and the acquisition of new competencies. Ultimately, staff members need to be made aware that it is in their best interests to support the change.

All projects have their critics. Those people who are important to the organization but unlikely to support the change should be distanced from influencing the project and should be confronted regarding any behavior that is critical of the implementation of the BICC.

> *Building familiarity with the BICC concept.* Building familiarity involves deliberately using stories, symbols, language, and training to get staff members familiar with the value, meaning, technology, and terminology of the BICC. Widespread and positive referencing of the project and its terminology conveys implicit support for the change; the more people hear the supportive language all around them, the more they believe in the reality and value of the change.
>
> *Maintaining and respecting continuity.* During the transition state, it is important not to criticize and discount the value of everything and everyone connected with the way things have been done up to now. By maintaining some sense of continuity, change managers can reduce concern about wholesale changes in power, authority, relationships, and core values.
>
> *Developing and communicating a clear picture of the future state.* Because staff members must have a sense of where changes are headed, it is important for the project leaders driving the change to be able to describe the future state with the BICC in place as fully as possible. The strategy developed at the outset of the project must include a thorough and targeted program of communication actions, including one-to-one, team, and organizational meetings, webcasts, and the use of other communication media such as newsletters, briefings, updates, etc.

Future Desired State. If the transition state has been managed effectively, the goal will have been reached. It is then necessary to confirm the point at which transition is complete and the change is implemented—when a BICC has been established and launched in the organization. However, the effectiveness of the new structure should be monitored against the performance criteria and ROI expected and established at the outset of the project.

Approach to Change Management

Every effort should be made to understand a company's requirements, by learning as much as possible about its business, history, structure, and culture, to help provide solutions that will be successful, especially when information on the current state and desired future state is acquired through the SAS Information Evolution Assessment.

Consultants should work with the company on both the strategic and operational level in these ways:

- Strategic level
- Operational level

Strategic Level. Strategic change factors stemming from your business environment and related goals will affect your mission and strategy, goals and objectives, leadership style, culture, infrastructure, work, people, and the levels of organizational performance you need to succeed. We set out to understand how a BICC can make a valuable contribution to the strategic change you desire. We also strongly recommend that Human Resources be proactively engaged in the Change Management process, as the Human Resources Department is most likely to be responsible for managing staff issues related to the changes required.

Part of this process involves our preferred position as both partner and team player who understands longer-term change processes, rather than as the provider of a single intervention to help tackle a specific problem or need. Our BICC concept supports this position as it focuses on helping you to develop into a BI organization as part of a strategic change process. Collaborating with management consulting experts might also be required, depending on the scope of the strategic change required and the ownership of the change agent role.

When involved in high-level discussions with your sponsoring executives, it is important that you ensure that you implement the BICC as smoothly as possible. Doing this includes highlighting the importance of Change Management and having the support from and building relations with your operational managers in IT, Business and Human Resources, who will be responsible for the change implementation processes you want to introduce.

Additionally, we gather and use the information on the anticipated effects the planned changes will have on your employees—for example, motivation, competencies, and training needs, attitudes toward SAS BICC implementation, and so forth—so we are better prepared to understand, interact with, and cooperate with your staff during the change process.

Operational Level. As mentioned earlier, the introduction of a BICC can directly affect a number of operational factors, ranging from organizational structure and systems, management practices, to individual performance and the working environment.

Often these operational factors are the ones most likely to directly confront consultants and trainers who are working on project implementation. This is where resistance, barriers, and problems might occur in establishing a BICC. It is important to ensure that your professional services representatives are prepared to understand and deal with:

- Issues around the acceptance of the solution or BICC
- Potential shortfalls or lack of adequate budgeting for BICC
- Reluctance to learn new skills
- Power issues and office politics
- Lack of motivation
- Lack of competencies
- Fear of the change itself
- Differences in organizational culture
- Exclusion from well-established teams
- Problems forming new project teams
- The working atmosphere generated by the change

Your consultant should make every effort to ensure that employees are equipped and trained on the professional, behavioral, and business level to help you introduce a BICC as smoothly and successfully as possible.

Making Change More Effective

It is clear that change is complex and that there is not a single solution. However, a number of key aspects emerge.

- A clear vision and strategy and effective leadership are key enablers as they provide the purpose, rationale, and drive for change.

- Appropriate and timely training is a key factor in implementing effective change.

- A clear communication plan is critical. Your employees' participation is an important enabler of change, especially in breaking down resistance. Human resource departments usually play a key role in change implementation.

- Finally, proactive Change Management plans and activities that bring together and tackle the changes to structures and infrastructures, work practices, people, and culture congruently can increase the chance of gaining successful outcomes, especially through the critical transition phase when you are implementing your BICC.

Summary

- The organizational culture is possibly the least tangible dimension. Within the context of this book, the term *culture* is defined as the moral, social, and behavioral norms of the organization's corporate environment, based on the attitudes, beliefs, and priorities of its members as it relates to the use and value of information as a long-term strategic corporate asset.

- An important prerequisite for the success of a BICC is to get organizational buy-in on the *use and value of information as a long-term strategic corporate asset.* So, to some extent, the organization needs to have bought in to this concept before it decides to set up a BICC. When the BICC is up and running, it will further foster and drive the importance of information in the organization.

- Achieving cultural change in the organization will no doubt be the greatest challenge for the BICC.

- Critical elements include:

  - A supportive reporting structure, that is, one that provides executive support and demonstrates top-level commitment to BI

  - A transparent funding model that demonstrates the BICC's value while making the cooperation with the BICC fair and flexible

- ○ Performance metrics that convey business value add
- ○ Knowledge Management processes that establish a culture of knowledge sharing and provide easy access to help and best practices
- All of these elements play a crucial role in gaining acceptance for the BICC and for the concept of BI in general.
- A setup process that goes hand-in-hand with a thorough Change Management approach stands the best chance of helping you integrate this cultural change into your organization.

ENDNOTES

1. More information about communities of practice can be found at: http://en.wikipedia.org/wiki/Community of Practice

2. Deloitte Research, "SAS: Trust and Respect—Rather than Command and Control," *Research Point of View: It's 2008: Do You Know Where Your Talent Is? Why Acquisition and Retention Strategies Don't Work*, 2004, 8,www.deloitte.com/dtt/.

3. Frank Leistner, "SAS Institute: Wissenmanagement am Beispiel einer Initiative zur weltweiten Nutzung von technischem Wissen: ToolPool" (SAS Institute: Knowledge Management Illustrated Using an Example for Worldwide Technical Knowledge Sharing: ToolPool), in *Corporate Knowledge—Durch eBusiness das Unternehmenswissen Bewahren* [Preserving Enterprise Knowledge through eBusiness], eds. Martin Schildhauer, Matthias Braun, and Matthias Schultze, (Goettingen: Business Village, 2003), 217–220.

4. Frank Leistner, "KM at SAS: The Power to Know," *Leading with Knowledge—Knowledge Management Practices in Global Infotech Companies*, ed. Rao Madanmohan (New Delhi, India: Tata McGraw-Hill, 2003), 419–445.

5. David Nadler, Michael Tushman, and Mark Nadler, *Competing by Design: The Power of Organizational Architecture* (London: Oxford University Press, 1997), 25–52, 181–203.

6. David Nadler, Michael Tushman, and Mark Nadler, *Competing by Design: The Power of Organizational Architecture* (London: Oxford University Press, 1997), 25–52, 181–203, and Thomas G. Cummings and Edgar F. Huse, *Organization Development and Change*, 4th ed. (St. Paul, MN: West Publishing Company, 1989).

Infrastructure

OVERVIEW

A Business Intelligence infrastructure needs to satisfy each business area's need for information of varying complexity and allow for a timely delivery up to near–real time if necessary. Therefore, on a high level, the key features of a BI infrastructure must:

- Support a diverse user audience with varying levels of skills and preferred information channels
- Enable all business users to obtain relevant information, from simple reporting to advanced analytics
- Allow for information to be available in the shortest possible time frame
- Allow for the BI strategy to grow and develop
- Support the use of information for decision making

Must these features be met before a BICC can be established? No.

It is important to emphasize that a BI infrastructure as just outlined should not be seen as a precondition for implementing a Business Intelligence Competency Center (BICC). In practice, the BICC will be instrumental in defining the future BI strategy for an organization and play an important role in the implementation or improvement of a BI infrastructure, at departmental and at enterprise level.

Depending on your current situation and on your overall strategy for the BICC, your selection criteria might equate only to a subset of the criteria for an enterprise BI infrastructure listed above: The key point is to plan for future growth and to strive to avoid creating insular solutions with no integration at all. The ideal BI infrastructure must allow for such a growth path: from a functional view and in terms of flexibility and sheer data volume.

Note: The term *infrastructure* refers to the hardware, software, networking tools, and technologies that create, manage, store, disseminate, and apply information.

CONSIDERATIONS FROM A
BICC PERSPECTIVE

The ideal BI infrastructure supports all functional areas of the BICC and allows it to operate in the most effective way, with minimum resources spent on everyday tasks and administrative overhead. Such a BI infrastructure would allow a BICC to work much more proactively with its diverse user community by freeing up BICC resources from day-to-day operations and basic maintenance work. Each one of the BICC's functional areas has specific requirements for a BI infrastructure; the sections that follow provide an overview of the key requirements for each area.

Business Intelligence Program

Right from the start, the BI infrastructure should not in any sense limit an organization's BI strategy. Looking ahead, the BI Program function will monitor trends and technologies that could further improve the organization's BI strategy; therefore, it is important that the BI infrastructure be extensible and open. The BI Program function needs to be able to satisfy the needs of business users in the most effective and timely manner. Thus, the number of resources spent on operations and maintenance must be as low as possible, in order to free up resources for work directly related to business demands.

Data Stewardship

Data stewardship is a key function within a BICC and indeed for the whole organization. Within this function resides much of the responsibility for accurate data and accountability. Therefore, this role is significantly eased by a BI infrastructure that has a built-in data quality solution. Such an infrastructure reduces the initial effort and pain in consolidating data from various sources to obtain a single quality view of the organization. Further, ongoing maintenance and future changes are eased by an integrated solution as compared to a one-off (ad hoc) data quality project. It is better to use an integrated approach where data quality routines are constantly applied than to make sporadic efforts to maintain data quality. Audits of any kind, whether internal or external/regulatory, can be executed with minimal additional effort.

Ideally, methods for data cleansing are incorporated into the BI infrastructure and are integrated with the overall data management.

Support

The workload on the technical and business-related support function directly relates to the level of comfort business users have with the BI tools they are using. This means that the tools need to be appropriate and easy to use and that the quality of the information must match user needs and expectations. Thus, ensuring that each user role has the most appropriate tool is essential and needs to be reviewed periodically and changed if necessary. User acceptance is boosted by a common "look and feel," by use of a consistent terminology, and, of course, by consistency of the retrieved information. Overall, the fewer resources the support function has to spend on basics, the more staff members are available to tackle the more advanced topics brought up by the user community.

BI Delivery

The audience of business users is diverse. Users have to be supplied with the tools that fit the task and that are appropriate for the skill level of a user group or profile. Implementing just a single tool might seem easier from a support point of view, but this approach loses much of its appeal when there is an increasing number of complaints about the tool being overly complicated or not powerful enough. Thus, a suite of BI exploitation tools is preferred, without sacrificing quality of information and consistency across these tools. This consistency can be achieved only via a common platform that allows, say, a point-and-click Web reporting tool and an advanced analytics application to share the same data and metadata. Further, such a platform provides a single point of control for access rights and other security matters. This point of control helps reduce implementation and maintenance effort of the applications suite, without limiting flexibility or affecting usability and user acceptance

Standard interfaces and application program interfaces (APIs) are essential, along with an integrated development environment. Business Intelligence delivery is further eased by the provision of functional blocks or services that are components of the BI infrastructure. Key examples are security, data acquisition, reporting and analytics services, and components that allow extending the platform but not circumventing it. Circumventing the platform is not desirable from many perspectives, including security and accountability.

Data Acquisition

The data acquisition function is quite literally at the heart of a BICC and indeed of any BI project. The challenge can be summarized by the familiar phrase "garbage in, garbage out." Without the optimum solution for data access, data preparation, and data cleansing, even the most advanced query and reporting tools will never actually tell you anything meaningful. Therefore, the BI infrastructure must enable the BICC staff to access virtually any data source in a timely manner and with reasonable effort. Predefined data models can help in the initial design and implementation phase, as they would give the organization a head start in identifying the necessary data for reporting and analytical needs. Finally, data acquisition is neither a singular nor an isolated event. For example, capturing daily (or even hourly) changes to the data requires a regular process; the need for traceability from the reporting or analytics application back to the source data requires interaction with other functions.

Advanced Analytics

Traditional query and reporting tools are able to provide only a rearview-mirror look. For a detailed analysis and for finding correlations and trends in vast amounts of data, a more sophisticated solution is required. This solution is commonly known as *data mining*. The mining process includes discovering previously unknown patterns (e.g., in customer behavior), building models using various modeling techniques and sample data, and finally deploying these models and running them against the full data (e.g., a customer database) to make predictions about future development based on that model. It is important to keep the motivation for data mining in mind: It is not about fancy math but all about solving a business issue using the most appropriate techniques. Therefore, any data mining solution has to allow for a business-driven approach, not merely a mathematical one.

Instead of being implemented as an insular solution, the analytics solution (data mining, but also forecasting and optimization) should be integrated with the BI infrastructure to improve collaboration between analytics experts and data integration specialists, between analytics experts jointly working on a topic, and between analytics experts and the business users. For a BICC, such a collaboration is essential as analytics solutions are going to be used both internally (i.e., the BICC offering them as a service) and also within business units (provided expert knowledge is available there).

Training

One of the issues with a diverse range of nonintegrated tools and vendors is the requirement to develop and maintain skill sets to support the individual pieces of the puzzle. It is important that skills can be reused, not only within the business user community, but also among staff members who deliver training.

A BI infrastructure provides a common terminology and standard definitions for data sources, metrics, business objectives, and so on, which makes working with different applications much easier for business users. Training does not have to start from scratch each time another application is used, which reduces training needs substantially. The same is true for the BICC staff implementing and maintaining the infrastructure. Further, training preparation can be simplified and common building blocks can be used.

Vendor Contracts Management

In a very direct way, resources necessary for the vendor contracts management function are linked to the total number of vendors that are involved in the BI infrastructure. From this perspective, it is desirable to keep the total number of vendors to a minimum—ideally down to a single vendor that is able to supply the whole BI infrastructure. Additionally, the degree to which a vendor is open to customer feedback is another factor here: Preferred vendors are those with an active and long-term customer relationship strategy. As the BI infrastructure normally will be implemented in iterations, it is desirable to have contractual conditions enabling the licensing of components (e.g., for data integration, reporting, analytics, and performance management) individually, without losing the benefits of integration.

Operational Support Systems for the BICC

Although not an integral part of the BI infrastructure, requirements for operational systems for a BICC are worth looking at. A natural decision is to use the BI infrastructure for all reporting and business management needs that the BICC has itself (e.g., performance management, budgeting), with the BICC thus becoming much like an end user itself. This way, skills can be reused and developed further, new techniques can be tested internally first, and, last but not least, a better understanding of business user requirements can be achieved. In short, a BICC should operate on the same standards as its customers' standards.

Other operational systems will be unique to the BICC but probably not unique in an organization. A call tracking system might already be available for the general service desk; sharing the same system also makes call handover easier (given a first-level support system that is carried out by your organization's general user service). Another important system is the knowledge database servicing the BICC staff and, if desired, business users too. Although it does not have to be necessarily a full-blown document management system, it must nevertheless enable its users to quickly search on combinations of keywords and store information in a variety of formats. Such a system (or a standard choice) might already exist in your organization.

Further important operational tools include project management and tracking, resource management and planning, general feedback and request channels (usually via the Web), and scheduling and registration applications for training and knowledge transfer workshops. Also, time and effort tracking systems, which are essential when the BICC's services are chargeable, are highly recommended, generally to identify support-intensive areas and topics. All of these can be standard off-the-shelf software or home-grown solutions, mainly depending on your organization's policies and standards.

BUSINESS INTELLIGENCE INFRASTRUCTURE SELECTION CRITERIA

To fully support all functional areas of a BICC and to ensure it operates in the most effective way, there are two major components of a BI infrastructure:

An enterprise intelligence platform—to achieve a single version of the truth

An industry framework—to achieve insight into all business areas

The first component, the enterprise intelligence platform, forms the solid foundation for an organization's BI strategy by seamlessly integrating components that span the whole information creation process, from data integration over dedicated storage to standard query and reporting and advanced analytics. Full transparency, traceability, and metadata integration facilitate the single version of the truth in accordance with business rules and regulatory requirements.

The second component, an industry framework, enables the organization to quickly extend the use of BI to various business functions and areas by providing industry-specific, ready-to-use logical and physical data models, data integration processes, analytical models, and standard reports.

The sections that follow discuss the key features for an enterprise BI infrastructure. A checklist is provided that can be useful for a first vendor evaluation. Even if you are planning to implement just parts of the functionality, it is advisable to plan for future growth and thus avoid a solution that has only a limited lifetime.

Integrated Components with Common Metadata

Rather than a best-of-breed approach, which often leads to a patchwork of various tools and products that are impossible to get to work with each other, the preferred way for building an enterprise BI architecture is to go for a suite of components that can be integrated with each other and that share a common metadata layer. This suite needs to span the whole information creation process, from data integration over dedicated storage to query and reporting and analytics. Only such a suite will allow a trace-back from report to source data and ensure data consistency ("one version of the truth") by a consistent use of technical and business metadata.

With integrated components, a lot of the administration effort previously spent on "making it all work" vanishes. Effort can be reduced further by establishing a single point of control for the whole BI infrastructure. Further, all security-related issues can be addressed centrally for all components, without the need to maintain multiple instances of access control mechanism.

All of the above functionality can be enabled by a metadata repository that is shared by all applications and tools across the BI infrastructure. Again, this reduces the maintenance efforts previously needed to make changes in multiple locations and allows all components to share and reuse metadata, such as business definitions, reports, and so forth. It also allows for a productivity boost on the business users' side.

Feature Checklist

- ☐ Integrated components covering data integration, dedicated storage, tabular and multidimensional reporting, advanced analytics
- ☐ Common metadata for all components
- ☐ Utilizing technical and business metadata
- ☐ Standardized, central management and administration tools
- ☐ Single point for security and access control
- ☐ Reverse impact analysis (trace-back) from report to source data

Scalability and Extensibility

With today's exponential growth of data volume and the anticipated much more widespread use of BI in organizations, any BI implementation will be challenged from both ends: more (source) data and more (business) questions to be answered from that data. Even with the best planning today, you cannot foresee the demand for future data volumes and business problems seeking answers. In fact, today you might not want to implement a BI infrastructure at all, with many resources not used until later in the life cycle. Further, you might plan to implement a BI Infrastructure in manageable chunks rather than in one large project. The answer to these challenges is "scalability and extensibility." *Scalability* means being able to meet future demands without having to retire an existing system and starting from scratch, and *extensibility* means allowing for a step-by-step implementation rather than a big bang approach.

Feature Checklist

☐ Scalable to future needs without redesign or retirement

☐ Scalable in terms of data, users, and information requirements

☐ Extensible to easily add and shift around workloads

☐ Support for a phased implementation, keeping cost and risks at minimum

Open and Standards Based

Even the most complete BI infrastructure will never be—and should never be—an isolated system. In simplest terms, data need to get in, and information needs to get out. Not all of this will be done within the BI infrastructure: Interfaces have to be available to other systems, such as security services, directory and user services, and a whole range of various, often in-house–developed applications. Further, distribution of information might include other tools, such as document management systems, enterprise communication systems, custom-written applications, and standard software for specific tasks. Not the least important is the ability to migrate, integrate, or even access legacy systems to the BI infrastructure on a data and metadata level.

Feature Checklist

☐ Interface with enterprise application integration products

☐ Supporting industry standards for exchange of data and metadata, and for communications

☐ Avoiding getting "locked in" by proprietary protocols and definitions

☐ Ability to integrate with existing systems, such as security and user directory services

☐ Following industry standards for data, metadata, and communications interfaces

☐ Supporting custom-built applications

Data Integration and Storage

Without the ability to integrate a vast variety of data sources and formats into a structured environment, any BI implementation will almost surely fail to provide fundamental benefits to the organization. The ability of a data integration solution to get to any data, on any platform, is an absolute must. Working around limitations is not only costly because of causing a high maintenance overhead, but also severely limits the capabilities to trace report figures back to their original sources. Data integration design is a complex task that can be eased significantly by using a visual design tool with the capability of supporting multiple users working on a project. Ongoing maintenance and change management tasks are eased significantly by extensive use of metadata throughout. In fact, one of the most important benefits of using a data integration design tool over handwritten queries and scripts is that it allows full documentation of every step and modification to the original data, for maintenance and for data transparency reasons.

It is important to understand the different requirements that BI and analytical applications have on data storage, compared to operational systems: Rather than moving little chunks of data almost constantly, BI and analytical applications might require an ad hoc sift through vast amounts of data in order to provide high-level information or to find trends. With BI, storage requirements are very much throughput-optimized, not transaction-optimized.

Feature Checklist

☐ Ability to integrate data from various source systems and formats

☐ Ability to access all computing platforms

☐ Easy-to-use, multiuser visual design tool and extensive use of metadata

☐ Advanced impact analysis and change management capabilities

☐ Specially designed storage products for use by BI and analytical applications

☐ Reduced overhead relational storage and multidimensional data storage capabilities

☐ Storage optimized for throughput rather than transactions

Integrated Data Quality Facilities

The ability to create the most visually appealing report is by itself pretty useless if the original data are of doubtful quality. Without a thorough data quality effort, a BI infrastructure is not complete. A direct link of the data quality functionality with the data integration component of the BI infrastructure is highly recommended to ensure that the data are clean and consistent, especially when data come from a variety of sources. Stand-alone data quality products, although providing some benefit in analyzing the data quality, will require significantly more effort when it comes to resolving the assessed issues. As they cannot provide direct handling of the data, often data export and import are required.

Feature Checklist

☐ Seamlessly integrated facilities for analyzing and resolving data quality issues

☐ Integrated data standardization and validation tools

☐ Support for your local standards of language, grammar, address structures, naming convention, etc.

Integrated BI Tools for a Diverse User Audience

The ability to cater to a wide variety of business users, ranging from a casual information consumer to an experienced business analyst and statistician, by providing fit-to-task interfaces is a must-have feature for any BI infrastructure. With the circle of BI users growing and becoming more diverse at the same time, this ability soon becomes one of the major criteria for success. A one-size-fits-all approach will leave a large part of the user audience with something too difficult to use for their needs and skills, while a significant part of the users will not be able to carry out their more complex tasks. Such a situation often leads to each group moving away from the common system and establishing side projects to meet their needs, thus increasing efforts for maintenance and decreasing reliability. The major advantage of having an enterprise BI infrastructure is that it uses a common set of standards, definitions, and data.

Feature Checklist

☐ Fit-to-task user interfaces and BI tools

☐ Common use of business definitions and business metadata across all tools

☐ Web and thin-client enabled

☐ Ability to interact with standard productivity tools

☐ Providing, or integrated with, a portal solution

Predictive Analytics and Modeling

The functional requirements for predictive analytics and modeling can vary, depending on the types of business questions that must be analyzed and resolved. The potential techniques include statistical algorithms, data mining, forecasting, and optimization techniques.

A powerful data mining solution for predictive analytics and modeling offers the ability to go from raw data to business-driven data mining models in a seamless process. This is accomplished by employing a large number of modeling techniques, an automated scoring process, an interface also appealing to nonstatisticians, and the ability to deal with huge amounts of data in a timely manner. Many low-end mining solutions are limited to a single modeling technique, such as decision trees. The real benefit, however, lies in having a solution that can employ and compare various modeling techniques, including neural networks, memory-based reasoning, clustering, regressions, and so on, and then pick the one that is best suited for the business problem. The actual model deployment is eased by automated scoring functions using a batch environment and parallel computing features.

Advanced analytical techniques benefit greatly from being part of an overall BI infrastructure. Detailed, nonsummarized data need to be extracted from source systems, often in an iterative process. A close collaboration between the data integration solution and the analytical solutions eases the process of data preparation significantly by sharing metadata, such as data definitions, column names, and so on. Further, common metadata allows sharing model definitions and results, thus improving collaboration between users and making results available for a wide audience.

Feature Checklist

- ☐ A graphical design tool to shorten model development time
- ☐ Support for a wide range of analytical techniques, including statistical analysis, forecasting, optimization
- ☐ Inclusion of a variety of modeling techniques, such as decision trees, neural networks, memory-based reasoning, clustering, regressions, associations, and time series
- ☐ Batch and parallel computing features
- ☐ Ability to deal with huge data volumes
- ☐ Ability to seamlessly collaborate with data integration, data quality, and reporting applications for easier data preparation

Tailored Business Solutions

All of the just-discussed selection criteria enable you to set up a solid enterprise intelligence platform upon which more specific solutions can be built—seamlessly integrated with the underlying platform. These solutions will address specific business areas, such as financial management, performance management, customer intelligence, risk management, and others. Although in principle all these areas could be addressed using generic tools and applications, it is much more cost effective to choose a prebuilt solution for, say, financial consolidation and reporting than to implement all necessary functionality by custom-written applications. Implementation time will be significantly shorter with a prebuilt solution too. Prebuilt solutions offer a familiar environment to the business user in terminology and functionality, which leads to higher user acceptance.

Feature Checklist

- ☐ Prebuilt solutions for key business areas
- ☐ Fully integrated into the underlying platform
- ☐ Appealing to the business user
- ☐ Full support for legal and accountability requirements

Prebuilt Industry Data Models

When implementing a medium- to large-scale BI infrastructure, a significant share of the effort is spent on designing and implementing logical and physical data models and analytical models. Although the details, such as source systems, table names, and availability of detail data, are dependent on the individual organization, the data and metadata that are collected and that are needed for analysis are remarkably similar within each industry. This fact allows for an industry-specific, generic data model that would, straight from the box, satisfy an organization's requirements to a large extent. Such industry data models benefit from their vendor's experience within a certain industry and offer a head start, compared to a data model designed from scratch, resulting in a reduced implementation effort and delivery time.

Feature Checklist

☐ Prebuilt logical and physical data models for your industry

☐ Prebuilt analytical models and reports for your industry and business area

☐ Fully integrated into the enterprise BI platform and business solutions

☐ Extensible to allow implementation of selected focus areas, with future addition of others

ROAD MAP TO IMPLEMENTING A BI INFRASTRUCTURE

Implementing a true enterprise BI infrastructure will occur most often in phases rather than in a big bang, and the implementation strategy will depend very much on your current situation. If your organization currently has a decentralized BI landscape, the major challenge in moving to a BI infrastructure is integration. If you already have a central infrastructure in place, you might want to check it against the selection criteria, evaluate it, and perhaps replace it step by step. Here, extensibility is the key criterion. Thus, to be able to set out any kind of implementation road map for a BI infrastructure, the most important criteria are:

- Integrated components with common metadata
- Scalability and extensibility
- Open and standards based

So how do you get there? First, identify your most critical issues. Then look for a solution but always keep the overall goal in mind: the establishment of an enterprise BI infrastructure. When you are evaluating a vendor, apply the whole set of selection criteria to understand how that vendor would fare in the big picture. Also, never underestimate integration issues.

The next sections describe scenarios and solution strategies to overcome the most common critical issues. Each describes an alternative route to the final aim of implementing a true BI infrastructure. Your situation might correspond to parts or combinations of these scenarios—or be totally different. In any case, it is highly recommended that you assess the situation with a trusted knowledgeable advisor in the field of enterprise BI solutions.

Scenario 1: Suffering from Poor Data Integration

For this scenario the overall pain, additional selection criteria (for the BI infrastructure), and functional areas (of the BICC) are:

- *Overall pain*

  Poor data quality and inconsistent data representations, often across disparate systems

- *Additional selection criteria*

  Data integration and storage, integrated data quality facilities

- *Business Intelligence Competency Center functional areas involved*

  Business Intelligence Program, Data Stewardship, Data Acquisition, Support

Potential Reasons for This Scenario. If you find yourself suffering from poor data integration, your most important task is to identify the reasons for inconsistency and mismatches. Often this is caused by a variety of extract/transform/load (ETL) tools being used, none of which can share any metadata with others and none of which is able to access all source data. The situation might be further complicated when a large amount of handwritten code is used, often to overcome the shortfalls of the ETL tools.

The Way Forward. Make the move from insular ETL tools to a true data integration solution, with integrated data quality facilities. Emphasize the importance of metadata usage for daily work and maintenance. Ensure that the data integration solution seamlessly integrates with specialized storage and, finally, verify that the solution is part of a platform concept and not simply a niche solution.

Scenario 2: Suffering from a Patchwork of Tactical BI Tools

For this scenario the overall pain, additional selection criteria (for the BI infrastructure), and functional areas (of the BICC) are:

- *Overall pain*

  Variety of nonintegrated tools that do not provide any benefit to business users, as reports and figures do not match up
- *Additional selection criteria*

  Integrated BI tools for a diverse user audience
- *Business Intelligence Competency Center functional areas involved*

  Business Intelligence Program, Data Stewardship, BI Delivery, Support

Potential Reasons for This Scenario. This scenario often is found when departments and teams have implemented their own BI products of choice, which can just about satisfy their own minimum needs. Still, some users in the department might not be satisfied, as the tool is not fit to their specific needs and skills, and they are discouraged to find out that different figures are used elsewhere in the organization, because a different tool might have been used.

The Way Forward. Move to a BI solution that offers a variety of tools and user front-ends suitable for different levels of skills and needs, all working on a common platform and sharing metadata definitions and standards between them. Verify that the BI solution is part of a framework to include data integration capabilities and advanced analytical features that share their metadata. Investigate whether solutions tailored for specific business areas are available.

Scenario 3: Suffering from an Inappropriate Data Model

For this scenario the overall pain, additional selection criteria (for the BI infrastructure), and functional areas (of the BICC) are:

- *Overall pain*

  Enterprise data model that does not allow exploitation by BI and analytical applications; major information missing or inconsistent
- *Additional selection criteria*

  Prebuilt industry data models
- *Business Intelligence Competency Center functional areas involved*

  Business Intelligence Program, Data Stewardship, Data Acquisition, BI Delivery, Advanced Analytics, Support

Potential Reasons for This Scenario. The reasons for this situation can be many: a jungle of different ETL tools with limited capabilities each, unmanaged growth and expansion of an out-of-date data model, new requirements for data that have been implemented in a quick-and-dirty approach circumventing an enterprise data model, or issues such as mergers and acquisitions or other substantial expansions of an organization's overall business.

The Way Forward. Look for a data model that fits your industry and that can be implemented directly into an enterprise BI platform, ideally by the same vendor to get around compatibility issues. Verify that the data model addresses not only data integration, but also query and reporting, online analytical processing (OLAP), and analytical models for various business areas. Finally, ensure that experienced staff members are available from the vendor locally to support the implementation in your organization and that iterative implementation is possible to keep the project manageable.

SUMMARY

- The BICC and indeed the whole organization benefit greatly from a state-of-the-art BI infrastructure. In short, such an infrastructure has two distinctions:

  1. A scalable enterprise BI platform with integrated components and a common metadata repository that enables access to all data

sources and features built-in data quality facilities, provides advanced analytical functionality, and allows the delivery of information to a diverse user audience via fit-to-task interfaces

2. An extensible industry framework with prebuilt data models and analytical models for your industry, seamlessly integrated with the enterprise BI platform, and providing tailored applications to address the major business areas and topics

- When implementing a BI infrastructure, keep the big picture in mind: Think big, start small. Select the area that is most important to you, and extend to include other areas later.

- Select a vendor not only on its ability to deliver BI technology but also other key criteria, such as corporate strength and stability, global reach and local presence, and, above all, customer commitment.

CHAPTER 9

Setting Up and Ensuring Ongoing Support

OVERVIEW

The previous chapters introduced you to the concepts you need to think about when setting up a competency center. But now, how do you get started? What process do you follow? This chapter introduces a suggested process for setting up a Business Intelligence Competency Center.

It captures the most important steps you would need to go through, starting with a high-level view of the implementation phases and drilling down to the specifics. (See Exhibit 9.1.)

EXHIBIT 9.1   BUSINESS INTELLIGENCE COMPETENCY CENTER SETUP: OVERVIEW

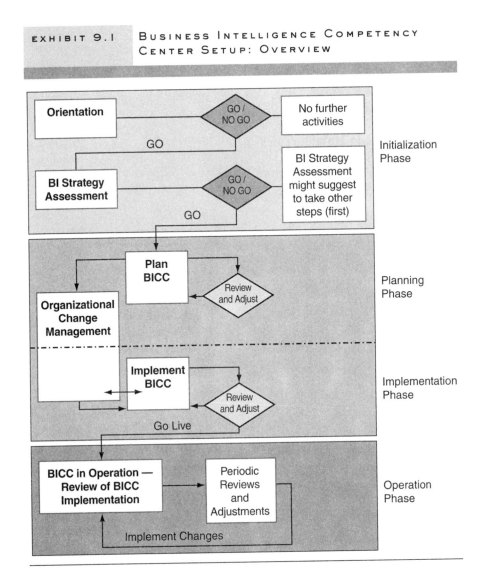

The BICC setup includes these phases:

- Orientation
- Business Intelligence.strategy assessment
- Planning
- Organizational Change Management
- Implementation
- Operation

SETUP PROCESS IN DETAIL

Managing the setup process of a BICC will be subject to many factors. The BICC concept will become more and more clearly defined as you are going through the process. It is very important that, when moving through the different phases of the setup, you set clear decision points for moving forward.

The following pages contain exhibits describing the various BICC setup phases in more detail. The exhibits highlight the major tasks that would be accomplished in these phases. The tasks will not always be worked through in exactly the sequence that is shown. Some of them will be going on concurrently. However, the exhibits provide a comprehensive overview of the tasks you need to perform when setting up your BICC.

For each of the tasks in the exhibit, we describe the content of that task, its outcomes, and its deliverables. We also give a list of the roles most likely to be involved in a particular task. However, for some of the tasks you might decide to bring in other individuals, including external providers, to help you facilitate workshops, provide advice and assistance on technical or organizational issues, and so on.

A section with some additional explanations and tips follows each exhibit.

Orientation. The first phase is about understanding the BICC concept and determining how it could move your organization forward. What is the primary goal? How should the BICC support the organization? What, on a high level, would it be tasked with? Who would be the sponsor? What would be the implications for the organization if a BICC were to be set up? Based on that information, you should perform an initial cost/benefit analysis for the creation of a BICC. Although you will not know all details for a cost/benefit analysis at this early stage, it is useful to collect any known costs or benefits now to decide if the setup of a BICC should be pursued or not.

You also should discuss the funding model for the BICC. You need to understand which funding model best suits the organization and its current culture. In this discussion, it is important to remember that putting a charge on the BICC's services should not deter business users. (See Exhibit 9.2 for details.)

EXHIBIT 9.2   ORIENTATION

The aim of the orientation phase is to introduce the stakeholders and other involved parties in the organization to the BICC concept and explore whether it has value for the organization. This could happen in a workshop format.

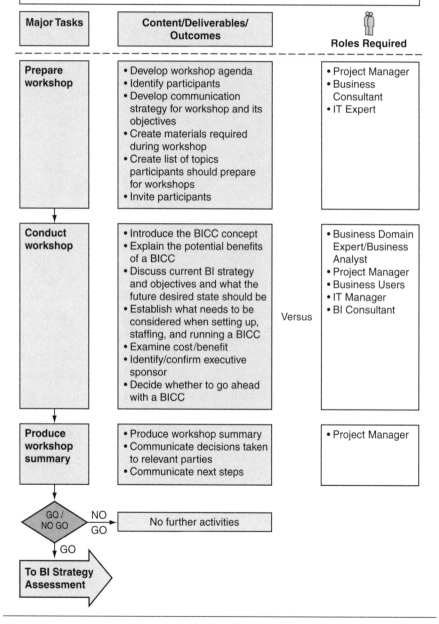

Major Tasks	Content/Deliverables/ Outcomes	Roles Required
Prepare workshop	• Develop workshop agenda • Identify participants • Develop communication strategy for workshop and its objectives • Create materials required during workshop • Create list of topics participants should prepare for workshops • Invite participants	• Project Manager • Business Consultant • IT Expert
Conduct workshop	• Introduce the BICC concept • Explain the potential benefits of a BICC • Discuss current BI strategy and objectives and what the future desired state should be • Establish what needs to be considered when setting up, staffing, and running a BICC • Examine cost/benefit • Identify/confirm executive sponsor • Decide whether to go ahead with a BICC	• Business Domain Expert/Business Analyst • Project Manager • Business Users • IT Manager • BI Consultant
Produce workshop summary	• Produce workshop summary • Communicate decisions taken to relevant parties • Communicate next steps	• Project Manager

Versus

GO / NO GO — NO → No further activities

GO

GO

To BI Strategy Assessment

Why orientation? It is important that everyone in the organization has a common understanding of what a BICC is and the purpose it serves. It is essential that you involve the "right" people from the start. Doing so helps avoid potential misunderstandings or issues up front, and your BICC stands a greater chance of becoming accepted and respected in the organization. Try to clarify as many questions regarding organizational structure, funding, sponsorship, BICC objectives, and mandate as early as possible. This will save time in the later phases. Collect any known costs that would be incurred and any known benefits that will be gained to lay the foundation for the BICC business case.

PHASE OUTCOMES
- Decision for/against a BICC
- Summary of anticipated benefits and risks involved in the BICC approach
- High-level cost/benefit considerations
- List of questions requiring clarification before/during BICC setup

Business Intelligence Strategy Assessment. In this phase, initialization continues. You should assess how information currently is used in the organization and how it should be used in the future. How the gap between the current and the desired state should be bridged needs to become part of a Business Intelligence road map. This road map outlines the strategy that the BICC should drive and support. All current and future BI projects should fit with this strategy. In addition to the road map, which outlines the mid- to long-term strategy, you should put together an action plan specifying the immediate actions to be taken. (See Exhibit 9.3 for details.)

EXHIBIT 9.3   BUSINESS INTELLIGENCE STRATEGY
                ASSESSMENT

The aim of the strategy assessment phase is to determine if there are any gaps between the desired and the current BI strategy.

Major Tasks	Content/Deliverables/ Outcomes	Roles Required
Initiate assessment and adjust scope	• Agree on the scope of required analysis • Develop assessment agenda • Identify participants • Develop communication strategy for assessment and its objectives • Create materials required during assessment • Create list of topics the participants should prepare for the assessment	• Project Manager • Business Consultant • BI Specialist
Conduct assessment	• Identify current and desired BI strategy • Perform gap analysis • Agree on recommendations • Define road map and action plan • Summarize preliminary results	• Executive Sponsor • Project Manager • Business Users/ Executives • BI Specialist • IT Management • Business Domain Expert
Review results with executive sponsor	• Finalize road map and action plan and implications for the BICC	• Executive Sponsor • IT Management • Project Manager
Decide on way forward	• Clarify funding, roles and responsibilities, next actions	• Executive Sponsor • Business Executives • Project Manager • IT Management

To Plan BICC

Why a BI strategy assessment? Your desire to set up a BICC might have many causes. One cause might be dissatisfaction with the current BI strategy or with the absence of one. The setup of a BICC creates a compelling event that should start with a review of how things are currently done and suggest required changes. Furthermore, a BI strategy assessment provides you with a 360-degree view of your organization and its BI requirements. If you do not review your current strategy at the time of the BICC setup, you risk having the BICC deliver results that reflect outdated BI requirements and expectations.

Finally, a BI strategy assessment will provide your BICC with a very clear mandate, a mid- to long-term road map, and a plan for immediate action. Thus, it is important that the assessment phase occurs before further BICC setup steps are planned in more detail.

In this phase, you will want to ensure that all relevant parties in the organization and their BI requirements are analyzed. A BI strategy assessment also provides the business users in your organization with an opportunity to provide input to the BI strategy. This approach will win you their buy-in for the BICC idea and also will generate interest for BI in general.

PHASE OUTCOMES
- BI strategy road map (mid-to-long term)
- BI strategy short-term action plan
- List of implications for the BICC

Planning. During this phase, you put together a detailed plan for setting up the BICC. The mandate and objectives of the BICC should be agreed on, based on the BI strategy assessment. You need to decide how the BICC fits into the organizational structure and how it is to be funded. The performance metrics for the BICC need to be agreed on.

You should now elaborate in detail the initial cost/benefit analysis performed during the initialization phase and build a formal business case.

The BI road map will also determine the functional areas that the BICC is supposed to cover. You should decide how those functions will be staffed and where the BICC reports within the organization. Also, you need to define the cooperation with other business units and external providers. (See Exhibit 9.4 for details.)

EXHIBIT 9.4   PLAN THE BICC

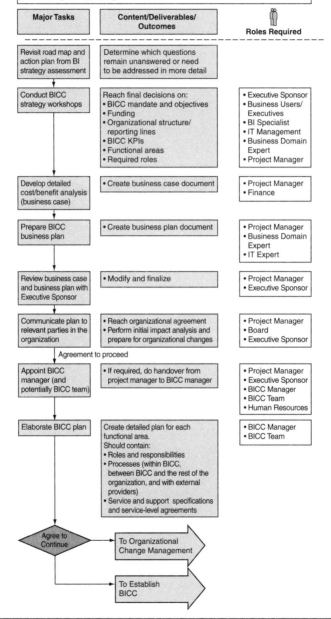

The aim of the planning phase is to work in detail through all the questions that need to be clarified before the BICC goes live. Planning the BICC is based on the agreed BI strategy. Some organizational change management activities should occur concurrently to the planning.

Major Tasks	Content/Deliverables/Outcomes	Roles Required
Revisit road map and action plan from BI strategy assessment	Determine which questions remain unanswered or need to be addressed in more detail	
Conduct BICC strategy workshops	Reach final decisions on: • BICC mandate and objectives • Funding • Organizational structure/reporting lines • BICC KPIs • Functional areas • Required roles	• Executive Sponsor • Business Users/Executives • BI Specialist • IT Management • Business Domain Expert • Project Manager
Develop detailed cost/benefit analysis (business case)	• Create business case document	• Project Manager • Finance
Prepare BICC business plan	• Create business plan document	• Project Manager • Business Domain Expert • IT Expert
Review business case and business plan with Executive Sponsor	• Modify and finalize	• Project Manager • Executive Sponsor
Communicate plan to relevant parties in the organization	• Reach organizational agreement • Perform initial impact analysis and prepare for organizational changes	• Project Manager • Board • Executive Sponsor

Agreement to proceed

| Appoint BICC manager (and potentially BICC team) | • If required, do handover from project manager to BICC manager | • Project Manager
• Executive Sponsor
• BICC Manager
• BICC Team
• Human Resources |
| Elaborate BICC plan | Create detailed plan for each functional area. Should contain:
• Roles and responsibilities
• Processes (within BICC, between BICC and the rest of the organization, and with external providers)
• Service and support specifications and service-level agreements | • BICC Manager
• BICC Team |

Agree to Continue

To Organizational Change Management

To Establish BICC

How to plan? The better you plan and the better you communicate your plan, the higher your chances for success. In this phase, you will want to ensure that the setup of the BICC is backed up by a detailed business case. Make sure you revisit that business case periodically to see how you are doing compared to your objectives. Related to that, you should put metrics in place that will prove the success of the BICC's work. These metrics can include cost savings reached through streamlining activities that previously have been done by different groups in the organization, leveraging skills in a more effective way, standardizing on software vendors, or gaining more business insight by increasing the use of BI, leading to cost savings or higher profit.

Buy-in and approval from the sponsor for the BI strategy is, of course, vital. Without a strong sponsorship for the BICC in the organization, the BI efforts will not get very far. If possible, sponsorship should be at the executive level and include buy-in from the business units as well as from information technology (IT).

It is important to agree on the roles and responsibilities—as well as service levels—so that user expectations are managed well from the beginning. How the BICC works internally and with other parts of the organization also needs to be defined to avoid duplication of efforts and unclear responsibilities.

PHASE OUTCOMES
- Clear definition of BICC mandate and objectives
- Agreed funding model
- Clear organizational structure and agreed reporting lines
- Metrics/key performance indicators (KPIs) for the BICC
- Agreed functional areas and their definitions
- Roles required for these functional areas and their responsibilities
- Detailed business case
- BICC business plan
- Defined processes within the BICC, with the rest of the organization, and with external providers
- Service and support specifications
- Basic information for developing the change management plan

Organizational Change Management. A BICC that constitutes its own organizational unit will result in people changing roles and responsibilities and have management implications as well. To implement these changes smoothly, a well-planned organizational change management approach is required. Therefore, both the planning and the implementation phases should be supported by a thorough change management plan. (See Exhibit 9.5 for details.)

EXHIBIT 9.5   ORGANIZATIONAL CHANGE MANAGEMENT

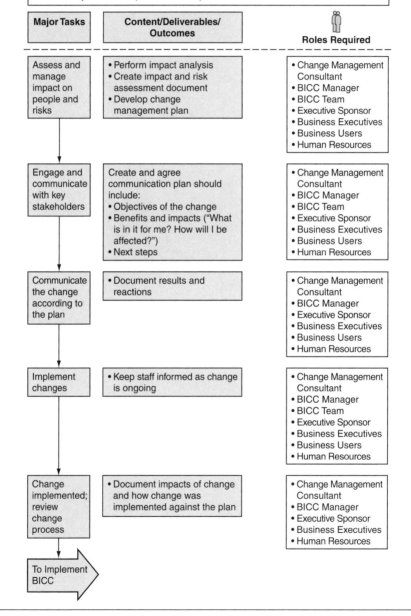

The aim of the change management phase is to support the organizational change caused by the BICC setup. Change management should start before the "Implement BICC" phase, preferably during the "Plan BICC" phase, and will be conducted concurrently with the "implement BICC" phase.

Major Tasks	Content/Deliverables/Outcomes	Roles Required
Assess and manage impact on people and risks	• Perform impact analysis • Create impact and risk assessment document • Develop change management plan	• Change Management Consultant • BICC Manager • BICC Team • Executive Sponsor • Business Executives • Business Users • Human Resources
Engage and communicate with key stakeholders	Create and agree communication plan should include: • Objectives of the change • Benefits and impacts ("What is in it for me? How will I be affected?") • Next steps	• Change Management Consultant • BICC Manager • BICC Team • Executive Sponsor • Business Executives • Business Users • Human Resources
Communicate the change according to the plan	• Document results and reactions	• Change Management Consultant • BICC Manager • Executive Sponsor • Business Executives • Business Users • Human Resources
Implement changes	• Keep staff informed as change is ongoing	• Change Management Consultant • BICC Manager • BICC Team • Executive Sponsor • Business Executives • Business Users • Human Resources
Change implemented; review change process	• Document impacts of change and how change was implemented against the plan	• Change Management Consultant • BICC Manager • Executive Sponsor • Business Executives • Human Resources

To Implement BICC

Why Organizational Change Management? The success of your BICC depends to a large extent on if and how this change was communicated to the people affected. Ensure that you communicate with and involve staff as much as is possible during the setup phases of the BICC. Every step along the way, it should be clear to members of the organization what is happening, why, what is in it for them, and how they will be affected. See Chapter 7 for more information about Change Management.

PHASE OUTCOMES
- Impact analysis and risk assessment
- Change Management plan
- Communication plan
- Documented results and reactions

Implementation. In this phase, the BICC team will be appointed, trained, and inducted to their jobs. Their work environment will be set up, and they will define the smaller details of cooperation within the BICC with other departments and external providers. The system to monitor the BICC's key performance indicators (KPIs) will be set up now. This is also the time when you communicate the kickoff and information on the BICC's first project to the rest of the organization. (See Exhibit 9.6 for details.)

EXHIBIT 9.6 IMPLEMENT THE BICC

The aim of the implementation phase is to prepare the BICC team for its new role, and to communicate the existence of the BICC to the organization. The tasks in this phase will not necessarily be completed in this order; some will occur concurrently. Also, organizational change management activities should run concurrently during the planning and implementation phases of the BICC.

Major Tasks	Content/Deliverables/Outcomes	Roles Required
Assign individuals to roles	• Appoint BICC team members (if this has not happened yet) • Create required competency profiles • Conduct training needs analysis • Create training plan for BICC team members • Train BICC team	• BICC Manager • BICC Team • IT Expert • Human Resources
Compile process handbooks and service-level agreements	• Write and publish process handbooks for each functional area (use input from detailed planning step in "Plan BICC" phase) • Write and publish service-level agreements	• BICC Manager • BICC Team • IT Management • Technical Writer • Business Users
Set up internal measuring process/ systems, assign budget, and outline details of funding process	• Establish measurement system and KPIs for BICC functions, services, and processes • Agree and publish funding process description	• Executive Sponsor • BICC Manager • BICC Team • IT Management • Finance
Prepare work environment	• Identify office space, order and stage equipment	• BICC Manager • BICC Team • IT and Operations Team
Identify first BICC project	• Identify first BICC project on the basis of the road map and action plan developed in the BI strategy assessment	• Executive Sponsor • Business Executives • BICC Manager • IT Manager
Kick off BICC	• People are inducted to roles/jobs • People have been trained • Communicate kickoff and details of first project to organization	• Executive Sponsor • BICC Manager

Go live

To BICC Reviews

How to implement? At this point, you will want to ensure that the implementation is going smoothly. To do that, select the right individuals to staff the BICC and prepare them for their roles. The first project will be a crucial one because it should demonstrate to the organization that setting up the BICC was the right decision. Therefore, select the first project carefully.

Ideally, the first project should have high visibility in the organization but also should have a very well defined and contained scope. These limitations will ensure that the project can achieve results relatively quickly. Selecting a highly visible project will ensure that large parts of the organization will learn about the existence and the successful work of the BICC.

When the operational BICC is positioned and announced in your organization, there are a number of important points to remember that will give the BICC a head start and ensure its recognition and sustainability in the eyes of the business lines. For example:

- Manage the expectations of the BICC and clearly communicate its goals and objectives. Sharing a common understanding of the focus and charter of the BICC is crucial to ensure that everyone is aligned on the stated priorities and deliverables.

- Ensure that the BICC projects are focused enough to show manageable, incremental benefits.

- Ensure that the organization is able to associate the benefit it is receiving with the services delivered from the BICC, for example, through a defined and transparent performance assessment process, visible organization communications channels, and a performance-based incentive system.

PHASE OUTCOMES
- Competency profiles
- Training plans
- Service-level agreements
- Documented processes
- KPI system in place
- Work environment prepared
- Staff inducted/trained
- First project identified
- BICC announcement

Operation. Starting with the first project, reviewing and evaluating the concrete benefits of the BICC are a must. Establish criteria to measure the BICC's success early in the planning phase and implement them as part of the BICC setup. Only when the BICC can prove its benefits will it be seen as an integral part of the intelligent enterprise and recognized for its achievements. A periodic review will also determine whether the responsibilities and scope of the BICC should be adjusted. (See Exhibit 9.7 for details.)

EXHIBIT 9.7   BUSINESS INTELLIGENCE COMPETENCY
CENTER IN OPERATION

The aim of the review phase is to revisit the setup and operation of the BICC and to make changes as necessary. The reviews should be conducted periodically.

Major Tasks	Content/Deliverables/ Outcomes	Roles Required
Measure KPIs and collect experiences	• Collect and analyze data • Revisit business case	• BICC Manager • BICC Team
Compile BICC status report and status report on ongoing projects	• Summarize how BICC does against business case • Create report on BICC performance and suggestions for improvements, changes, and new plans • Publish project status reports on an ongoing basis	• BICC Manager • BICC Team
Agree on changes with Executive Sponsor	• Discuss changes and their implications with Executive Sponsor	• BICC Manager • Executive Sponsor
Implement changes	• Document agreed changes • Inform BICC team and other affected parties in the organization • Update process handbooks, service-level agreements, and other documentation • Communicate achievements to the organization • Execute next plans	• BICC Manager • BICC Team

Why review? It is important to review how the implementation went for everyone involved to find out what could be improved. Address issues that were caused by the organizational change now, if you have not done so yet. Otherwise, they will remain unresolved and create problems in the future. Also carefully review the mandate, business plan, and business case to see if the BICC's scope should be adjusted, to determine if the BICC "endeavor" lived up to expectations, and to be clear on the achievements. Likewise, also periodically review the projects conducted by the BICC.

PHASE OUTCOMES
- BICC performance report
- Project status reports
- Documented agreed changes
- Updated documentation

WORKING WITH SOFTWARE VENDORS

What to Look for in a Vendor

In Chapter 8, we discussed what the BICC needs in terms of BI software to best serve its business users. Although infrastructure is key, there are also other important indicators to take into account when deciding on a particular vendor. For the BICC, the capabilities, commitment, quality, support, and reliability of a vendor are instrumental to its being able to deliver to the business. In selecting the appropriate BI software vendor, consider the following factors. Each will play a key role in your cooperation with the vendor of that software.

- Comprehensive BI platform
- Advanced analytics
- Organizational reach
- Global reach and local presence
- Corporate strength and stability
- Customer commitment

Comprehensive BI Platform. As opposed to a point solution or packaged application, a *comprehensive enterprise BI platform* provides a complete, integrated, scalable framework for identifying and collecting organizational data and for converting data into accurate, timely BI. By definition, an end-to-end BI platform includes elements for planning, data integration, intelligent storage, query and reporting, and advanced analytics.

True business insight is about more than making smart investments in individual technologies. It is about what happens when those individual technology areas come together into a synergistic system. Business Intelligence success does not just happen at the application layer. It depends on a chain of applications and technologies working together from a common data foundation to create a single, verifiable version of the truth.

A comprehensive BI platform integrates individual technology components into a single synergistic system. Information flow can then transcend functional silos, organizational boundaries, computing platforms, and specialized tools. Decisions can be made rapidly, with full knowledge of underlying context and hidden interdependencies.

Advanced Analytics. Beyond historical query and reporting tools that merely tell an organization where it has been, *advanced analytics* includes sophisticated technologies that incorporate predictive capabilities, including data mining, text mining, forecasting, and optimization.

In an uncertain economy, companies need to be able to predict and manage customer demand, not just react to it. They need to understand how, where, and why costs are being incurred in order to model the impact of cost savings and changes to business processes. Without predictive modeling, it is difficult or impossible to quantify the impact of business decisions.

Organizational Reach. *Organizational reach* refers to the depth and breadth of the solution's applicability, where *depth* refers to serving users at all levels of the organization (providing appropriate interfaces and tools for quantitative analysts, business users, and executives) and *breadth* refers to sharing BI across functional areas and to a broad (and mobile) audience.

Typically, a business process involves both analytical and business users—people whose backgrounds and needs are so different that IT has difficulty satisfying all their needs. Quantitative specialists need to explore and fine-tune the analytic foundations, but their colleagues might simply need to see or report on the results, without having to understand the underlying analytic processes.

A BI solution should empower business users to create their own actionable, strategic intelligence, while quantitative users have the flexibility to fine-tune models and IT retains control over data integrity. The results of these analyses should be easily disseminated across all functional areas and organizational levels so everyone can promote the organization's success.

Global Reach and Local Presence. *Global reach* means that the vendor has corporate offices in major markets and a global communications process for customer services and support across all your international locations. *Local presence* means the vendor's products are localized and that the vendor has a high percentage of employees who are local citizens and speak the local language.

The BI vendor that offers global reach and local presence is able to consistently serve global markets and organizations while maintaining a high level of personalized, local customer service. With global reach, your organization receives consistent services and support across all locations, strengthened by the vendor's access to global resources and global best practices, plus domain expertise based on many engagements worldwide.

With local presence, the BI vendor can mobilize quickly to respond to local issues and understands local market conditions, regulations, and compliance issues.

The organization's geographic scope is one indicator of its strength and stability. The established BI vendor that has a significant global footprint is likely to be in a more solid financial position than the start-up vendor that has limited geographic reach.

Corporate Strength and Stability. *Corporate strength* means the vendor shows consistent revenue growth and profitability over time and operates on a strong and predictable revenue model. *Corporate stability* means that the vendor reinvests generously into research and development (R&D), retains key talent, and is not plagued by layoffs or downsizing.

Investing in BI solutions is a major commitment, and your BI vendor should be a strategic supplier for the organization. The wrong choice entails major risks. What would you do if your BI vendor were forced to scale back product development during lean times, were acquired by another organization that has divergent directions, or, worse, went out of business?

The recent flurry of mergers and acquisitions among BI vendors has sparked some well-deserved concern. The newly formed entities will claim the advantages of their converged resources, but often the merger actually does little to reduce the size and complexity of the customer's IT portfolio; key talent has been lost in the process, and the vendor must devote significant time and resources to the inevitable problems of dovetailing two companies. A track record of corporate strength and stability is a good indicator that the vendor is not only big enough to serve your complex, multilocation organization but that it will be there tomorrow. And when an organization is consistently profitable, it can weather economic downturns and continue to focus on meeting customer needs and investing in technology innovation.

Customer Commitment. *Customer commitment* is shown through such activities as customer user groups, postsale technical support, and customer relationship development and recognition—and is marked by customer loyalty shown through customer annual renewals, repeat business, and goodwill among customer IT staff.

Experts agree that customer service is just as important as the product itself in gauging a BI vendor. Enterprises make huge investments in BI, and critical corporate objectives depend on BI success—objectives related to corporate productivity, profitability, and viability. You need assurances that your BI vendor prioritizes customers' needs (and, in turn, the value of your BI investments) over its own short-term internal initiatives and financial targets.

Appropriate levels of customer commitment result in quality software releases that have been shaped by user feedback, premium technical support and professional services, and, ideally, a direct relationship where the vendor accepts clear, one-to-one accountability for the provided solutions and the customer relationship as a whole.

The next section examines criteria for evaluating customer commitment.

How to Evaluate a Vendor's Commitment to Customers

A considerable part of the BICC's success depends on its "ability to deliver." This ability, in turn, is highly dependent on how well the BICC is able to rely on the support it is getting from the software vendors it works with.

These vendor capabilities are crucial for the success of the BICC:

- Business and industry expertise
- BI strategy consulting
- Implementation consulting

- Training needs analysis
- Comprehensive and customizable training offering
- Certification program
- Publications
- Internal marketing and user group support
- Technical support

Business and Industry Expertise. The vendor you work with should have a thorough understanding of your business and industry and should supply you with professionals who have experience in your specific industry. Equipped with both an in-depth knowledge of BI and practical field experience in your industry, the vendor and its partners should be able to support management throughout the evaluation, purchasing, and implementation phases of BI software, and beyond. It is important that any engagement start with identifying your specific business needs, issues, and key objectives to evaluate alternatives. Also, the vendor should assist your business units and financial managers in building a business case for your investment and support you in determining the need, scope, and benefits you might receive from a BICC.

BI Strategy Consulting. "The ability of the vendor to form a positive relationship with the BICC will have an impact on their success in supplying and assisting the organization."[1]

Most important, a vendor needs to understand the concept of a BICC as well as understand and fit into the BICC's strategy. If desired, a vendor should be able to assist the BICC with shaping that strategy. A vendor that is merely focused on technology and does not understand how to create a sustainable environment that ensures the technology investment pays off cannot be considered a strategic and reliable partner for the BICC. The vendor must understand the BICC concept, have a view on how to staff the BICC, understand the required competencies and functional areas, and be able to leverage off a wide network of partners.

Implementation Consulting. It is important that the vendor has at its disposal a comprehensive pool of expert implementation consultants, either within its own organization or through access to highly qualified partners.

From a BICC point of view, it is particularly important that, throughout the service engagement, expert consultants share their knowledge and real-world experience with your staff so they can then manage the results of the project independently. Here are specific implementation services that could support a customer in establishing or operating its competency center:

- Implementing service-level agreements and IT invoice management solutions
- Implementing enterprise warehouse and BI solutions
- Expert advisory services

Training Needs Analysis. The goal of a training needs analysis is to determine the competency gaps that exist in the organization and to recommend means of overcoming these gaps. The current knowledge level of the organization's team (with regard to their own jobs and project roles as well as with the company's business goals) is examined. The analysis examines the difference between actual and desired competence.

Training needs analysis is the first part of the training cycle. It is very important for ensuring a successful training outcome, as it takes the business, project, and individual learning and development goals into account while the training is planned. This approach ensures that training is fine-tuned to the organization's needs. A training needs analysis also should define the criteria for analyzing the results of the training (outcome analysis).

A vendor should ensure that a training needs analysis precedes the delivery of training to your BICC or business users. A training needs analysis shows that the vendor has a professional approach to training and understands the training requirements of your staff. You should be confident that the vendor will deliver training that is customized to your needs.

Comprehensive and Customizable Training Offering. Although a vendor should be in a position to cover a very broad range of topics, it should be able to focus in depth on the specific topics that are required by your staff, customized to your needs. The offering should include possibilities for public as well as custom-made courses, workshops, and seminars that use your data and address the context in which your staff members work. Also, knowledge transfer or coaching sessions are useful for getting individual members of your staff up to speed quickly.

The vendor should also be able to offer you multiple delivery methods that are designed to meet your time, budget, and learning style requirements. Examples could include live-Web classes and self-paced e-learning or a combination of instructor-based and self-paced learning in a blended learning approach.

Quite often, software vendor training tends to be quite technical. For many business users, the question is: How can technology help me to solve my business problem? For example, how can I implement a Balanced Scorecard solution in my organization? How can I use data mining to maximize my profit of customers? A comprehensive offering would include training on business- and industry-specific topics and about how they can be solved using technology. Business user training requires a good understanding of your business processes and issues on the part of the vendor. It is important for the BICC that the vendor be able to adapt to different target audiences.

The commitment to offering exceptionally high levels of teaching skills among individual trainers is essential. The vendor should have a quality assurance process in place to ensure that the training is delivered by instructors who are experts in the subject matter and who are monitored and mentored continually in their instructional skills.

Certification Program. Throughout the business world, companies recognize that certification is the way to stay abreast of the latest technology and serves as a benchmark for hiring, promoting, and planning employee career paths.

The individuals who work in a BICC represent a pool of experts with a proven track record of expertise in their subject matter area. Certification is a reliable instrument to ensure that staff members have the required knowledge to perform in their job roles. Certification programs offered by software vendors help you to ensure that this knowledge is kept up-to-date and remains at a consistently high level. Likewise, the presence of a certification program helps you to differentiate the most qualified technical professionals, increase individual and group productivity levels, and improve your organization's overall competency using the software.

Publications. In addition to the part they play in a comprehensive training program, books and periodicals from a vendor can give you greater insight into the vendor's offering and can answer very specific questions that you might have when using the software.

Internal Marketing and User Group Support. Internal marketing is essential for a BICC. As it is new to the organization, other business units need to hear about its existence, its objectives, and its activities. Furthermore, it is part of the mandate of the BICC to educate the organization about the value and the possibilities of BI. Here, vendors can be of help by supplying information, holding information sessions on specific topics, or providing marketing material or other publications.

Many competency centers organize user groups within their organizations to raise awareness for BI and the BICC's work, to keep the community informed about latest trends and technologies, and to share experiences. Vendors can support you in that effort by supplying speakers, material, and logistical support for your user group.

Additionally, it is very beneficial for BICC staff members to attend public user group meetings, organized by vendors or independently, to stay abreast of the latest developments in the BI software industry.

Technical Support. Good cooperation with a vendor's technical support group is essential for the BICC to provide quality services and support to its own user community. Issues should be resolved as quickly as possible, and knowledge about how the issues were resolved should be retained effectively by the BICC, using knowledge management techniques, to be accessible in the future.

Our recommendation is that first- and second-level support should be taken care of by your organization itself. The BICC should refer any third-level support tracks (i.e., those that could not be solved in-house) to the vendor.

Exhibit 9.8 shows you how technical support for BI tracks could be handled.

Summary

- Implementing a BICC requires careful planning. The main points are these: Be clear about the goal, obtain executive sponsorship, find the right staff, and involve and communicate with all stakeholders.

- Sometimes it is politically difficult to drive this change without external help. But you can work with management consulting firms, system integrators, and software vendors to get advice and assistance at each step.

EXHIBIT 9.8   TECHNICAL SUPPORT INVOLVING THE BICC

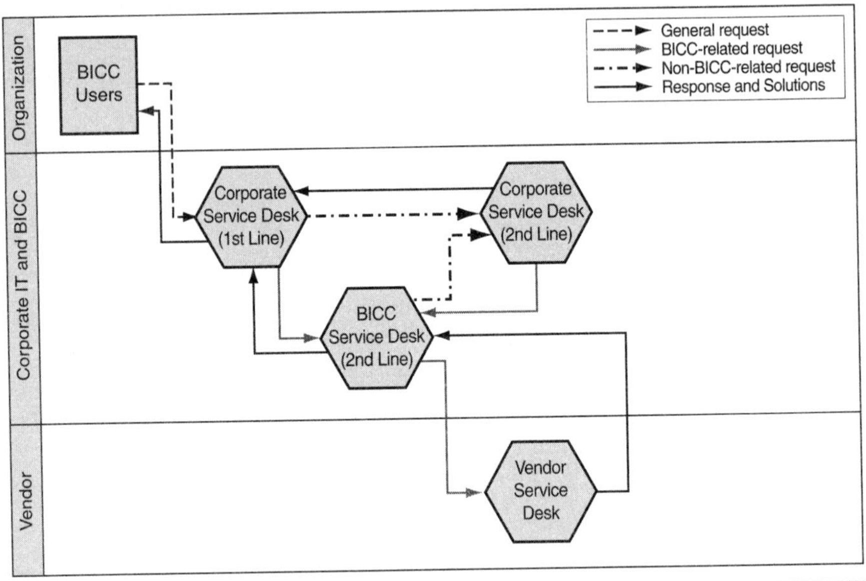

- When you select software vendors, select them not only for their technology, but also for the customer commitment they demonstrate.

ENDNOTE

1. Alan Tiedrich, "The BI and Data Warehousing Tools Selection Process—A Recipe for Success," *Proceedings of Gartner Business Intelligence Summit*, London, 2005. 8.

Cases from the Field

This chapter provides you with information on how some companies have set up their Business Intelligence Competency Centers, what their motives were, and what they think is important to focus on while implementing a BICC. Read about their experiences in the cases they have written to share with you.

INSURANCE, SOUTH AFRICA: MUTUAL & FEDERAL DEFINES BUSINESS INTELLIGENCE STRATEGY

This case concerns Mutual & Federal (M&F), one of the leading insurance companies in South Africa. M&F provides insurance service to the personal, commercial, and corporate markets. It operates in the marketplace through professional brokers who are able to offer clients personal service and advice when purchasing policies and practical assistance in the event of a claim.

In 2003, M&F together with SAS embarked on a strategic program that was tasked to implement an enterprise-wide management information solution using the SAS Insurance Intelligence Solution. Ownership for this initiative was held at top executive level. A project management board met every month to monitor progress on this strategic program. The board members were all individuals from the general management team representing the business units of the organization. The first deliverable consisted of implementing analytical solutions. During the first phase of the project, M&F realized that, in order to make its focus on creating both the infrastructure for reporting and the environment for building a strategic business intelligence (BI) program operational in the organization, it would need to have a structure that would provide a sustainable environment for advocating the usage of BI.

The primary objective for the BI department is to achieve "one single version of the truth" across all reporting mechanisms by transforming data into knowledge, which will enable decision makers to make effective and informed decisions. In order to achieve this objective, the pooling of business, information technology (IT), and analytical skills into one department is essential. This central department will ensure that the development and implementation of standardized BI processes is achieved across the enterprise. This department is responsible for providing training and end user support and will provide the expertise when advanced analytics, data acquisition, and warehousing development functions are required.

SAS was instrumental in helping M&F define its BI strategy and set up the BI department. A management consulting firm was also involved to address the organizational change management aspects that went along with the creation of the BI department.

PUBLIC ADMINISTRATION, ITALY: CSI-PIEMONTE MANAGES GROWTH WITH A BUSINESS INTELLIGENCE COMPETENCY CENTER

Since 1977, CSI-Piemonte has promoted innovation in the public administration sector through the use of modern IT and Internet tools. As a provider of BI and IT platforms to the public administration of the Piedmont Region, CSI has included SAS in its solutions since 1980.

In the last 20 years, the Piedmont Region, using technologies from CSI-Piemonte, built a substantial information asset (850 databases, 500 collections of information, about 20,000 tables). Since 1996, this important information base has been organized in sectorial data marts that contain historical and integrated information concerning different domains of activities (tourism, instruction, health, agriculture, environment, cultural heritage, demography, justice, etc.).

"We count on SAS to support projects in a wide variety of areas," explains Guido Albertini, the director of International Projects at CSI. "For instance, we've supported the Piedmont Region with its healthcare planning policy. We track and observe pharmaceutical prescriptions, monitor epidemiology and oncology activity, and we provide a number of human resource management and budget optimization solutions for the regional public sector."

With more than 70 BI analysts and developers, CSI delivers SAS solutions to thousands of end users throughout Piedmont's public administration offices. According to Albertini, "CSI uses SAS solutions to develop the largest part of the regional decision-making information system, which helps the public administration managers to provide vital information such as budgetary forecasts and revenue analysis."

"Our Business Intelligence area has considerably grown in the last few years, because data warehousing, Business Intelligence, balanced score-cards, and statistical solutions are indispensable to politicians and decision makers who need to measure activity and prepare forecasts for the future," explains Albertini.

As more and more of the Piedmont Public Administration began to rely on CSI's SAS solutions, the company saw a need to create an internal organization to support its users. "Since the SAS activities were growing quite quickly, it became necessary to create an internal organization with some structure," says Albertini. "So we decided to implement our competency center and we had some advice from SAS on how to do it."

CSI's competency center offers help through a centralized call center that can dispatch SAS specialists by phone or in person throughout Piedmont. The competency center's staff also communicates regularly with its customers' data centers, and it manages all software products within its applications.

"We have a number of skilled people who are dedicated to providing internal and external consulting and support the use of the applications," says Albertini. "So this fits quite well with the ideal competency center organization that is proposed by SAS. And today we are glad to have reached a very good practice level in SAS®9 platform and solutions."

According to Albertini, the competency center has enhanced CSI's efficiency and discipline as a service provider. "The main benefit has been a better use of resources," he says. "There has been an important growth of activities because public administration is investing very much in the modernization of its information systems. So we had to be organized to follow that growth. Our competency center has helped us to become more organized and more customer-oriented as we've managed that growth."

BANKING, BELGIUM: KBC BENEFITS FROM AN SAS BUSINESS INTELLIGENCE COMPETENCY CENTER

An SAS customer for more than 20 years, Belgium's KBC Bank & Insurance Group relies on SAS for dozens of data mining, data manipulation, and BI applications throughout the company. With more than 200 SAS developers and nearly 1,000 end users for its SAS applications, KBC needed a way to centralize its support for SAS users.

According to KBC's Yves Roelandt, the need for a BICC became clear in 1998, when Kreditbank, ABB-Verzekeringen, and Cera-Bank merged to form the current KBC Group. Roelandt heads KBC's competency center.[1]

"After the merger, it was not always clear who was responsible for the SAS software itself or what was built with the SAS software," explains Roelandt. "Each firm had an explosion of users, and often you didn't know who your users were. Everything became more complex. Therefore, we set up an organization, together with the users, to have a clear view of who was doing what with SAS."

At KBC, SAS applications are developed and maintained within the company's business units where the domain expertise resides. But the support for those developers and their end users comes from the BICC. The mission statement for KBC's BICC gives Roelandt and his team responsibility for maintenance and upgrades on all SAS products, control over the SAS BI environment, and consultancy support to all users of the BI platform.

Roelandt's team includes 14 consultants who comprise both a maintenance and a project team. The maintenance team provides user support from a help desk model and ensures operational continuity of the SAS environment. The project team implements infrastructure projects and handles all upgrades and changes to the existing SAS environments.

"Once you choose a certain platform for Business Intelligence, it's logical to have all the competence for that environment centralized in one team," says Roelandt. "If your users don't know where to address their problems with a certain tool, then you need a competency center. If your vendor is receiving questions or negotiations about products from several different areas in your organization, that's also an indication that there is a need for a competency center."

"I think all companies with a certain number of users and large SAS environment can benefit from creating a competency center," concludes Roelandt. "Having that single point of contact is important both for your internal customers and your vendor relationship."

BANKING, SOUTH AFRICA: COMPETENCY CENTER DRIVES RETURN ON BI INVESTMENTS AT NEDBANK

Nedbank Limited is one of South Africa's largest financial institutions with $45 billion on its balance sheet (2004) and a retail customer base of 3.1 million customers. Its branded businesses include Nedbank, Old Mutual Bank, Pick 'n Pay Go Banking, and American Express in South Africa.

In 2002, Nedbank Retail built an SAS data warehouse to provide an integrated view of the customer based on information collected from its transactional systems. This enabled the company to start cross-selling more effectively to its customers, and these successes led to a demand for the rapid implementation of SAS in other areas of the business. But it is one thing to have the technical infrastructure in place; you also need people with the right mix of technical, analytical, and business skills to make the most of world-class BI software. It became increasingly clear to Nedbank that it needed to establish an SAS BICC.

The BICC has now been in existence for more than a year, and currently employs nine staff with specialist skills in data analysis, business analysis, and management information systems. Simon Marland, chief information officer at the Nedbank Retail division, explains the rationale behind the BICC. He strongly believes that the IT function has a strong responsibility to deliver value to the business and to show that it is delivering value. "The CFO [chief financial officer] and CIO [chief information officer] need to measure ROI [return on investment] and see the direct financial benefits of their investments in technology.

"We have built an excellent data warehouse over three years with 45 terabytes of data, 28 data marts, and a range of advanced applications serving 9,000 users. The challenge was to maximize the return on the investment, and we decided that a federal IT support model was critical to achieving this objective. It would enable us to integrate all of our SAS applications, which of itself brings major productivity gains, and to adhere to IT standards while putting business benefit first, enabling us to achieve quick but sustainable wins on projects large and small. So in pursuit of this objective we set up a BI Competency Center alongside the other competency centers at Nedbank. The main point of having such a center of excellence is that it enables project managers to quickly identify individuals who can add a lot of value to their projects."

"The challenge in establishing a BICC is to recruit people who offer the right skills, behavior and competencies! SAS helped us a lot in building our assets—it has fantastic knowledge, not just about the technology but more importantly the world of banking. And its reach extends worldwide—SAS is one of the best examples of a global village!" says Marland.

SAS and Nedbank worked on a gap analysis to establish what skills were lacking and a program for individuals to round out their skills.

"Once you have found the right people, a competency center is the ideal place for them to work, as they get the opportunity to contribute to projects across the group and serve the requirements of 9,000 users. Often these projects cut across departmental boundaries, so this gives the individuals space to grow," says Marland.

Summary

- Many organizations are seeing value in setting up a BICC.
- The most successful companies plan thoroughly for BI and create a sustainable environment that amalgamates business and IT perspectives and competencies and centralizes the BI experts in the organization to best leverage their skills.
- They provide a transparent structure with clear roles and responsibilities that efficiently and effectively supports the business users and that helps drive BI to more users in the organization.

Endnote

1. Yves Roelandt has since taken on a different role in the company and has been replaced by Mark Baudemprez.

CHAPTER 11

Ten Recommendations for a Highly Effective Business Intelligence Competency Center

According to a February/March 2005 survey from Better Management entitled "How Do You Plan for Business Intelligence?" 60 percent of the respondents say they never, rarely, or only sometimes get the information they need to make effective business decisions. Those with intelligent enterprises want to make sure that everyone throughout the organization is making fact-based decisions to mitigate risk and maximize performance.

Evolving the intelligent enterprise is a complex task that requires promoting and supporting the use of information for decision making at all organizational levels. A central structure, such as the Business Intelligence Competency Center, for defining, executing, and supporting the Business Intelligence strategy, ensures the robustness, sustainability, and reliability of the information infrastructure and, at the same time, enables heterogeneous groups of information consumers to use information in a coordinated way to achieve the organization's goals.

This book has provided an overview of the BICC concept and its benefits and given recommendations for setting up and maintaining a BICC. It has highlighted the most important aspects you need to consider when implementing a BICC. So, what is it that will distinguish an effective BICC from an ineffective one? How will you know you are there? What are the key points to consider?

Have a Vision for Business Intelligence

Executive management has to buy in to the idea that information is a highly valuable corporate asset and needs to be managed as such. Management needs to believe BI can be used to drive the business forward. Management must make this support visible to the rest of the organization by giving executive sponsorship to the BICC concept and by assigning the BICC a prominent and influential place in the organization, where it can operate with authority. Management needs to commit to a culture of fact-based decision making.

Create a Joint Venture Between Business and Information Technology

The BICC needs to act as a broker that brings together business understanding and technology expertise. In many organizations, communication between business and technology is difficult. The BICC, by definition, tries to provide intelligence to the business. It needs to translate business questions into technology and the answers back to the business. Doing this requires knowledge and skills on the business and information technology (IT) as well as on the analytical side and the communication and people skills necessary to promote efforts, evangelize results and solicit feedback and participation.

It's a Process, Not a Project

The BICC should be there to stay. It should not be treated as a project with a start and end date. Integrating BI into the business will be an ongoing process, and the organization will never feel all its BI needs have been addressed. As business requirements change, there is a constant need for more advanced, or "a different kind" of intelligence. An intelligent enterprise will become increasingly accustomed to fact-based decision making and will want to use information in more and more of its business processes.

Maintain Clear Vision, Concrete Objectives

As with all initiatives, be clear when defining what you want to get out of setting up a BICC. The vision needs to be such that all affected parties in the organization understand and subscribe to it. To achieve organizational buy-in and implement the vision, it is important to define measurable and realistic objectives that are transparent to all stakeholders as well as the BICC and that translate into concrete short-term achievements that prove the tangible value of the BICC.

Integrate and Consolidate

The BICC should oversee all BI-related initiatives on an organizational level and guard against overlap, redundancy, and information silos. It needs to be involved in defining the overall BI strategy to ensure that the approach to BI shifts more and more from tactical to strategic. It should evaluate which tools and technologies are fit for the purposes of the organization and drive standardization efforts while ensuring it is enabling the needs of the business.

PRACTICE EFFECTIVE CHANGE MANAGEMENT

Change is the only constant, and the acceptance of change is greatly increased by a thorough Change Management plan that caters to the impacts of the change and highlights its benefits and risks. The ultimate goal is that all affected parties buy in to the change, realize what is in it for them, and are enabled to deal proactively with any potential problems or conflict resulting from the change. An important point here, in order to get buy-in and support, is to involve affected individuals as much as possible in the BICC setup by including them in a BI needs analysis and keeping them informed as the setup process progresses. All stakeholders should be a part of the process. They must have an opportunity to communicate their needs as well as receive regular updates and information.

CARRY OUT STAFF INDUCTION, TRAINING, DEVELOPMENT

For the BICC to hit the ground running, it is essential that everyone in the BICC team is very clear on roles and responsibilities and how they relate to other departments. Clear processes should be in place to avoid conflict and duplication of effort. Based on the roles and responsibilities of BICC staff members, a training needs analysis should be performed to understand their training and development requirements. A training assessment will also be required for the business users.

DELIVER ONGOING VALUE

Once the BICC is set up, it must demonstrate its value to the organization on an ongoing basis. This value needs to be communicated constantly to the organization as vocally and visibly as possible. Performance metrics should be defined as part of the BICC's setup process, and these metrics should be monitored to see how the BICC achieves against them. The overall goal of the BICC should be to provide ongoing value to the business by supplying the intelligence needed to achieve corporate objectives. The business should perceive this value at all times. Therefore, an effective communication strategy is a vital part of the BICC's work, where the center talks about its projects, successes, plans, and achievements.

Ensure the Infrastructure's Depth and Breadth

A BI infrastructure needs to satisfy and support each business area's requirements for information of varying complexity and allow for a timely delivery of that information. The BICC should provide an infrastructure that enables a diverse user audience with varying levels of skills and preferred information channels and helps all business users to obtain relevant information, from simple reporting to advanced analytics. The infrastructure should enable the BI strategy to grow and develop over time and allow for sharing BI across functional areas.

Use a Multidimensional Approach

Last but not least, successful BICCs understand that BI is not just about technology. First-class infrastructure needs to be combined with highly skilled people, transparent and efficient processes, and a culture that fosters fact-based decision making. The BICC should therefore work on all these dimensions in unison to turn the organization into an intelligent enterprise.

Information is one of the most valuable assets of your organization. Capitalize on your investment in your infrastructure, people, and processes by developing and operating a highly effective BI support center for your entire organization.

List of Abbreviations

AI	Analytical intelligence
API	Application program interface
ARPU	Average revenue per user
BI	Business Intelligence
BICC	Business Intelligence Competency Center
CDI	Common document index
CEO	Chief executive officer
CIO	Chief information officer
COO	Chief operating officer
CoP	Community of practice
DBA	Database administration or administrator
DWH	Data warehouse
EMEA	Europe, Middle East, and Africa
ESDB	Employee skills database
ETL	Extract, transform, load
HR	Human resources
IEA	Information evolution assessment
IEM	Information evolution model
IT	Information technology
KM	Knowledge Management
KPI	Key performance indicator
LILA	Learning and Innovations Laboratory
Mgmt	Management
OCM	Organizational Change Management
OLAP	Online analytical processing
PSD	Professional Services Division
RACI	Responsible, accountable, consulted, informed
RAD	Rapid application development
RFID	Radio frequency identification
RFP	Request for proposal
ROI	Return on investment
SD	Service desk

AI	Analytical intelligence
SLA	Service-level agreement
SOW	Statement of work
SPOC	Single point of contact
TCO	Total cost of ownership
TNA	Training needs analysis

Additional Roles

Exhibit B lists the roles that could exist within the Business Intelligence Competency Center (in addition to the roles mentioned in Chapter 5), be covered by other business units, or be outsourced to an external provider. Some of these roles will definitely be covered by other business units (e.g., Finance) but will support the BICC in its activities.

An electronic version of the complete list of roles can be downloaded from the BICC book Web site. See the Preface for details.

EXHIBIT B.1 ADDITIONAL ROLES

Job Role	Source	Role Description
Advisor to the Legal Department	Business	Acts as a contact for the legal department and provides input on the content of Business Intelligence software-related agreements and licenses.
Board of Directors	Business	Acts as the body that has to approve substantial investments and make decisions that affect the entire organization.
Business Domain Expert	Business	Acts as subject-matter expert for a particular business area.
Business Executive	Business	Is accountable for the operative business of a division or department.

(continues)

Job Role	Source	Role Description
Business Users (or End Users)	Business	Interact with the data warehouse and BI solutions to obtain necessary information for their day-to-day decision making. Advise the BICC on business and usability requirements. Are involved in testing and signing off on solutions.
Executive Sponsor	Business	Defines the BICC's objectives in relation to the organization's objectives. Also identifies the key individuals involved in setting up the BICC, establishes priorities, and authorizes and sponsors the BICC setup. Also responsible for establishing and monitoring escalation procedures to be taken in the event of conflict. The sponsor must have a strong influence on the organization as a whole since the BICC setup is likely to have an impact across functional units.
Finance Officer	Business	Provides support for putting together a business case for the BICC and implements cross-charging for the BICC services.
Human Resources	Business	Involved when organizational changes concerning personnel (changes in job, role, etc.) are planned and executed. Performs career planning, succession planning, job grading.
Construction Manager	IT	Coordinates the construction process and performs interviews, requirements analysis, and design to ensure that the application meets the business objectives.
Data Manager	IT	Manages the corporate data model, providing data standards, naming conventions, and data quality. Provides information on the design of the operational data sources and is responsible for reviewing and approving the subject data models, dimensional data models, and physical data models.

Job Role	Source	Role Description
Data Quality Specialist	IT	Assesses the data and resolves all data quality issues by working with the data manager and business analyst. Performs all necessary tasks related to assessing data quality, preparing the data quality resolution strategy, and customizing the quality knowledge base. Performs parsing, match coding, merging, and defining the quality index on source and target data. Is an expert for specific data quality software and implementation issues.
Enterprise Information Manager	IT`	Positions BI as a competitive advantage and ensures that the organization leverages off its BI investment. Ensures the establishment and maintenance of an appropriate BI strategy to meet the organization's information needs. Ensures the establishment of processes to define, integrate, and synchronize data across the organization (data governance). Drives and champions initiatives to address data quality with the relevant business owners. Coordinates strategy and business rules governing data security and information storage, thus ensuring regulatory compliance. Establishes a process to monitor adherence to the defined strategy and business rules. Manages data as an information asset.
IT Manager (and IT and Operations Team)	IT	Advises the BICC team on the organization's overall IT strategy and coordinates the appropriate IT staff to support the BICC team. Is responsible for the ongoing operations, maintenance, and administration of the IT environment.

(continues)

Job Role	Source	Role Description
		Each individual project requires a variable degree of IT and Operations staff support. Group roles, responsibilities, and the number of individuals necessary will vary from organization to organization. Therefore, no specific role is indicated for most IT and Operations personnel here. Individual IT managers can best determine which roles and individuals are needed. Typically these roles will be required: • IT architect • Operations manager • Application developer • Network administrator • Systems administrator • Hardware specialist • More technical specialists as necessary In this book, the term *IT manager* is used to refer to the IT manager or any member of the IT and Operations team.
Project Security Specialist	IT	Provides the project team with information on all aspects of security, including security infrastructure, rules for accessing source data, and restrictions (if any) for accessing and using derived data.
Quality Team	IT	Performs quality assurance and quality control activities, including testing. The team can contain employees of the organization and might contain service providers and third-party members. The review members of this team, as well as their review processes, are defined during the project. Quality specialists (representing various areas of quality in the organization), business users, business analysts, and IT are usually members of the team.

Job Role	Source	Role Description
Technical Communicator	IT	Identifies, plans, and produces documentation supporting the BICC. Communicates effectively with people from diverse technical and business backgrounds.
Warehouse Administrator	IT	Uses knowledge of operating systems and data language to maintain the warehouse effectively, including scheduling and monitoring refresh jobs and managing disk space and utilization.

Index

DATE DUE
